STORY BRIDGES

PRACTICING ORAL HISTORY SERIES
Series Editor:
Nancy MacKay, Mills College

Museums, historical societies, libraries, classrooms, cultural institutions, alumni associations, and neighborhood groups are among the growing list of organizations who use oral history to document and change their own communities. This new series will fill the gap in oral history research and practice by providing concise, instructive books that address the special circumstances of oral history practiced outside the academy. Each title will provide practical tools for conducting and presenting an oral history project that conforms to the best practices of the Oral History Association while being accessible to community-based organizations who use oral history methods.

Volume 1:
Story Bridges: A Guide for Conducting Intergenerational Oral History Projects, Angela Zusman

STORY BRIDGES

A Guide for Conducting
Intergenerational Oral History Projects

Angela Zusman

Left Coast
Press Inc.

Walnut Creek, California

Left Coast Press Inc.

LEFT COAST PRESS, INC.
1630 North Main Street, #400
Walnut Creek, CA 94596
http://www.LCoastPress.com

ISBN 978-1-59874-424-8 hardcover
ISBN 978-1-59874-425-5 paperback

Library of Congress Cataloging-in-Publication Data

Zusman, Angela.
  Story bridges : a guide for conducting intergenerational oral history projects / Angela Zusman.
     p. cm.
  ISBN 978-1-59874-424-8 (hardcover : alk. paper) -- ISBN 978-1-59874-425-5 (pbk. : alk. paper)
  1. Oral history--Handbooks, manuals, etc. 2. Intergenerational relations. 3. Families. I. Title.
  D16.14.Z87 2010
  907.2--dc22

                    2010021826

Text Design by Angela Zusman,
www.uniquelyperfect.com

Printed in the United States of America

⊖™ The paper used in this publication meets the minimum requirements of American National Standard for Information Sciences —Permanence of Paper for Printed Library Materials, ANSI/NISO Z39.48–1992.

CONTENTS

For Tootsie

ACKNOWLEDGEMENTS

The story of *Story Bridges* is filled with amazing, helpful and inspiring people. Thanks first of all to the Oakland Asian Cultural Center and all the participants in the Oakland Chinatown Oral History Project, especially Anne Huang, for your support, insight, and collaboration. To Nancy MacKay, the angel of oral historians, for so generously sharing your knowledge and doing everything you can to support the process of oral history making. To Glen Whitman, Howard Levin, Gigi Yang, Shifra Teitelbaum, Julie Norko, and all the youth participants for sharing your wisdom and experiences. To the Association of Personal Historians for creating a foundation of support, and knowledge for personal and oral historians. To GC, the light of my life and the source of my inspiration. To Kevin and Sasha for gracing me with family. And most of all, to my grandparents Hy, Mickey, Louise and Claire for showering me with love, inspiring my curiosity, and instilling in me a sense of pride, confidence, and respect for life and all its stories. This book is for you.

The Value of Stories

Under the Earth I go,
On the oak leaf I stand.
I ride on the filly
That was never foaled,
And I carry the dead in
my hand.

—Anonymous; traditional storyteller's introduction

If there is one thing all human beings have in common apart from their biology, it is stories. Stories are loved, told, remembered and retold by humans of every age, gender, tribe and point in history.

When I was young, I liked nothing more than to settle back into my grandmother's ample bosom and listen to her tell me, yet again, the stories of my father's childhood. My sister and I preferred the naughty stories of course, especially the one about the night Grampa came home from World War II and was greeted by his two-year-old son, whom he had never met before, announcing that he had just set the bathroom on fire. Aside from being a family heirloom, this story also nicely illustrates oral history. It combines an historical event with personal circumstances. While thousands of books have discussed the end of the war and the fact that soldiers returned home, most of them do not include any details about what occurred once the door to that home had been opened. These stories are found only in the memories of those who experienced them, and the only way to find them is to go directly to the living source.

Why are stories so powerful? In 2003, the International Journal of Information Technology and Management published an article defining four principal reasons.

> "First, stories are universal, crossing boundaries of language, culture and age. Second, they mirror human thought. All evidence from neurology and psychology leads to the conclusion that humans think in narrative structures. Concepts conveyed in story form—more than ideas explained with logic and analysis—imprint themselves naturally into human minds. Third, stories define who we are. Our sense of identity is forged by the stories we tell ourselves, the ones we come to believe and those we choose to dismiss. Fourth, stories build and preserve a group's sense of community. Stories align and motivate by portraying the world in vivid terms that build emotional connections among constituents, giving them a sense of shared purpose."[1]

In essence, stories transcend time, space, culture, and even truth. Events take place but once, reverberating ever after in the form of a story. We dream in stories. Our memories come to us as stories. Our senses lead us straight to stories. The smell of the sea reminds us not just of the ocean as an object but of our relationship with the ocean: hot summer days; hands sticky with melted ice cream and grains of sand; the feeling of awe as we contemplated jumping into those big waves; mom's voice calling us in, again and again, to come eat lunch; getting wrapped in a

---

1. Loick Roche and John Sadowsky, "The power of stories: a discussion of why stories are powerful," *International Journal of Information Technology and Management 2003*, Vol. 2, No. 4, p. 377.

big soft colorful towel; laying in the hot sand to warm up enough to jump back into the ocean again. One scent, infinite stories. Many have said that it is through stories that we make sense of our world. I propose that it is through stories that we also remember and make sense of our lives. Our stories tell us who we are.

Stories also teach us where we come from. The old photo on the wall means nothing until I am told that the young unsmiling girl is my great-great grandmother and this is the only surviving photo of her—indeed, the only picture at all from our ancestors' centuries in Russia. Now, the picture is dear. I search for my features on her face. I wonder what she was like, and hope that she was happy. Even this tiny fragment of a story has brought this photo to life, bringing my great great-grandmother with it.

"Don't wait. Don't tell the story later. Life is so short. This stretch of sea and sand, this walk on the shore, before the tide covers everything we have done." These words from novelist Jeanette Winterson convey both the impermanence of our existence and the potential immortality of stories. She warns us to act with haste. The untold story disappears with its silent narrator. The thread goes underground. Years ago, when viewing my great-great grandmother's photo, I could have asked one simple question: What village is that? But I did not, and neither did anyone else. Now the elders with those stories have gone and I must work very hard to resurrect them. For most of us, it is all but too late.

Still, I was very lucky. All four of my grandparents lived within miles of my family so I have years and years of overlapping stories to keep me warm and rooted. Through their stories I learned that I come from a long line of hardworking people who were able to overcome incredible hardship and still laugh, dance, share, and enjoy a good noisy meal together. Through their actions I learned to respect the past, thrive in the present, and create and believe in a brilliant future. Their collective love and stories created a foundation from which I set out confidently to explore this world. It was curiosity, not emptiness, which propelled me onward.

What have you learned from your elders? What do you wish you knew?

Many young people today live very far from their family elders. The well-documented fragmentation of the American family has uprooted individuals from their shared history. We start afresh with each generation instead of drawing upon the wisdom of our inheritance. Young people are left to themselves to figure out who they are by looking only forward. Elders are left with their attics full of stories, cobwebs multiplying with their sense of uselessness. Yet each generation has so much to offer the other.

The elder who tells the story is granted an audience, a sign of respect for what they have to offer. Each question, asked with interest, acts as a key, unlocking the relevance that had been seeping away from them with age. The young person stretches outward, connecting words with their own experience; the world becomes a tiny bit more inspiring and manageable. In the alchemy of storytelling, they both transcend time and space. The questioner and narrator become two sides of one coin. Through this process, the story of the elder is bequeathed to the youth, its new keeper. This book is an attempt to elucidate this process of sharing and preserving stories so they can continue to teach and inspire others, an endeavor called oral history.

HOW TO USE THIS BOOK

Some years ago, I was managing an intergenerational oral history project and struggled to find books and resources to guide the process. I was able to patch together information from a variety of sources but a book with all the details would have saved us a lot of time and attempts at recreating the wheel. This book is an attempt to provide all the information you might need to conduct your own project. It can also serve as a guide for any team members who are not familiar with oral history. In addition to the "how to" elements, there are several case studies to exemplify the different avenues other projects have explored. These examples are set aside from the main text so you can easily find what you are looking for.

The case studies are drawn from five very different projects from around the country. Interviews were conducted with project directors, volunteers, and youth participants to showcase a range of viewpoints and experiences. Some of the featured projects are oral history projects in every sense, from preparation to archiving. Others employ some of the steps in the process. They were selected to present a range of options so that you can get ideas that will work for you and your community. The goal here is not to stipulate what you must do, but provide guidance for what you can do. The table on the following pages offers some details about each project.

At the end of the book, there is an appendix with resources such as sample forms and documents that can be adapted for your specific needs.

Oral histories provide researchers with important data. They bridge communities by bringing people together around a common theme. They resurrect dying practices and languages, almost-forgotten events and rituals. For those who participate in such projects, they also remind us of our collective humanity. We learn from each other; we come to respect our differences and find unexpected places of unity. Oral history is where people and history meet.

Why should stories matter to you? Whether you are hoping to document a particular event or collect vignettes about a particular place, whether you consider yourself a historian or a student, an expert or a novice, an important person or an innocent bystander, there is a place for you in this cycle as well as a benefit you can create for the world.

Everyone wonders what happens to them after they die. Here on earth, they become stories.

PROJECT TITLE & SPONSORING INSTITUTION	PROJECT GOALS	PROJECT SUMMARY	YOUTH PARTICIPATION
Telling Their Stories: Oral History Archives Project --- **PRIVATE HIGH SCHOOL**	Engage students in history; learn skills such as interviewing, shooting and editing film, and building websites	Students conduct interviews, create films and online archives	Junior and Senior students manifest entire project as part of curriculum
Oakland Chinatown Oral History Project --- **COMMUNITY CENTER**	Document local history; connect generations	Youth volunteers interview local elders and archive interviews	Youth volunteers conduct interviews, create transcripts, support event
Fusing Identities --- **LIBRARY**	Increase local history collection; provide engaging youth activity	Youth and local elders cross-interview each other to learn history and find their similarities and differences	Youth volunteers initiate and conduct interviews
Life Storytelling Program --- **SENIOR RESIDENTIAL COMMUNITY**	Document residents' life stories; improve quality of life	Volunteers interview residents and create life story synopses	Some youth volunteers conduct interviews and write synopses
youTHink --- **YOUTH AFTER-SCHOOL PROGRAM**	Educate youth about local and family history; learn interview skills	Youth interview their family and learn about local history and migration patterns	12 - 17 year old after-school program participants conduct interviews and research

Figure 1: Oral History Case Study Details

Archiving Method	Means of Access	Public Element	Time line	Impact
Partial edited transcripts with video clips	Website	Ongoing events	Semester-long program ongoing for 10 years	Decrease discrimination; increase positive contribution to society.
Complete oral history packages in university collection, libraries and community center	Libraries, website, sponsoring institution	Ongoing exhibitions and public events for each new phase	Ongoing; Now into Phase 4. Phase 1: 18 months	Increase community awareness and support of center and community legacy
Edited and unedited DVDs of all interviews	Local cable channel, middle schools, libraries	Video premier for participants and families	One school year	Increase library's local history collection; deepen bonds in community
Story synopses bound and given to resident, family, and library	Library of sponsoring institution	None	One month per resident; ongoing program	Residents feel validated; caregivers provide better care
6 - 8 minute audio recordings kept at sponsoring institution	Internet download, local museum audio tour, sponsoring institution	Some stories added to museum's audio tour	One school year	Deepen connections between family members and different cultural groups; increase confidence

CHAPTER ONE

History and Benefits
of Oral History

One lesson we can learn from pre-industrial peoples is the power of storytelling. I am struck by how important storytelling is among tribal peoples; it forms the basis of their educational systems. The Celtic peoples, for example, insisted that only the poets could be teachers. Why? I think it is because knowledge that is not passed through the heart is dangerous: it may lack wisdom; it may be a power trip; it may squelch life out of the learners. What if our educational systems were to insist that teachers be poets and storytellers and artists? What transformations would follow?

—Matthew Fox

Oral history is both a process and the product this process creates. The process takes verbally transmitted information, generally in the form of structured interviews, and converts it into a product that can be preserved and shared. The product that is preserved and shared, also called an oral history, can take many forms. The primary source created from an oral history project is the recording of the interview itself. This can be an audio or video recording, or both. Secondary sources or products represent the content from the recording and can include transcripts, edited films, websites, books and other documents and mediums.

As expressed in the previous chapter, there are many uses for oral histories. The completed oral history serves as a valuable historical document. By creating an oral history, you are creating a primary historical source—a snapshot of history that comes directly from the participant.

Oral history differs from other story-collecting ventures, such as journalism, because of its emphasis on preservation. Like a journalist, an oral historian may do research, conduct a structured interview, and create a report based on what was learned. While the journalist may be satisfied with the publication of their article, the oral historian goes one step further by preserving the actual recording as well as the product that comes from it. This distinction is important because it highlights the importance of archiving for the oral historian, a facet of oral history that is less familiar to those who may embark upon such a project.

All of this describes what oral history is. What is it not?

Oral history is not an attempt to define an objective "Truth". Instead, oral history exposes the truth as expressed by each narrator. With oral history, truth is relative. Two people may have two opposite ideas of what is true. One might say, "He was a great man," while the other deplores him. They may remember events, circumstances and even the weather very differently. In this way, oral history can be compared to quantum physics. As with particles, events are also affected by the act of observation. One cannot observe a quark without affecting it, so no two observations are the same and neither can be considered True. In the same way, no event can be experienced or recollected exactly the same way by two different people, and neither recollection can necessarily be deemed more true that the other. One narrator's favorite event can be another's worst nightmare; one man's success can be another man's failure. Opposing or contradicting recollections are often both true.

Still, fact checking is important. Many people mix up dates and even locations of important events. Some mistakes need to be corrected; still, the focus of oral history is the narrators' memories more than any consolidated idea of Truth.

THE HISTORY OF ORAL HISTORY

"The story—from *Rumplestiltskin* to *War and Peace*—is one of the basic tools invented by the human mind, for the purpose of gaining understanding. There have been great societies that did not use the wheel, but there have been no societies that did not tell stories."

—Ursula K. LeGuin

Oral histories have been collected since communication began. For many cultures, verbal transmission was and continues to be the most important method for passing down and therefore preserving ideas, rituals and histories. As early as 1100 BCE, emperors of the Zhou dynasty ordered scribes to record oral histories "for the benefit of court historians."[2] In the fifth century BCE, the Greek historian Herodotus collected first person accounts of the Persian Wars. The African tradition of *griot* and the Jewish tradition of *zahor*, which means active remembrance, emphasize not only the telling of stories but the importance of passing them down from generation to generation. Later, in the 19th and into the 20th centuries, historians became more interested in a scientific approach to history, one that focused on things as they "really" were. This methodology presupposed only one truth, however, and disregarded the many personal experiences revolving around a single event. By the middle of the 20th century, interest shifted from historical elites to the lives and experiences of "ordinary" people. Oral histories were conducted to uncover incidents from the battlefield to the workplace.

---

2. Rebecca Sharpless, "The History of Oral History", *History of Oral History*, AltaMira Press, 2007, p. 9.

In addition to historians, activists used oral history to build foundations for their causes, such as the civil rights movement and labor activism. Communities invested in their own local histories and folklorists collected stories and songs. Today, thousands of books and articles teach the methods and share the fruits of oral histories. Several universities offer academic degrees in oral history and some, such as UC Berkeley, house their own oral history collections. The Library of Congress maintains an enormous and growing collection of oral histories, and new projects spring up every year in all corners of the world. Perhaps this is because oral history truly is history for and by the people.

In today's age of sound bites and the relentless accumulation and distribution of minutiae, the oral history process—with its in-depth focus and appreciation for the whole story—is perhaps even more important. The technological advances that underpin this so-called "Information Age" are creating shifts in our society and culture that portend rapid, ongoing change in everything from how individuals spend their resources to how institutions deal with data and even how countries address the needs of their populations. Oral history allows us to embrace change without losing precious experiences, lessons, details and wisdom of the past.

INTERGENERATIONAL ORAL HISTORIES

An intergenerational oral history goes one step further than a traditional oral history by specifying exactly who participates. This form of oral history brings together people of different generations, generally youth and elders, for the purpose not only of collecting stories but also creating a bridge between generations. In addition to contributing to history, this story bridge opens up new worlds for both parties. As opposed to the passive learning that comes from reading history books and other secondary historical resources, oral history is very engaging and hands-on, making it an excellent learning and teaching medium for people of all ages. Moreover, oral histories provide glimpses into worlds most often neglected by traditional historians. Everyday lives, sentiments, and reactions to historical events bring the past to life in ways that textbooks or even great documentaries cannot. Many of these experiences have never been written about, so the only way to learn about them is to find a primary source.

Nothing compares to sitting with a person as they tell you about their own experience. While secondary sources such as films and history books are extremely valuable, no film or book can replicate the feeling in the air or the connection that is forged between the narrator and interviewer. These stories will be remembered far longer than those studied for the sake of passing a test. These stories inspire curiosity instead of sating the mind with facts that become irrelevant once the book is put down or the test completed. The telling of these stories also allows for contribution from people who have the most experience and the least opportunity to contribute. Preservation of this material is a gift to society that simply cannot be matched by the secondary sources created through traditional research.

Oral history includes the heart and the guts of the stories in addition to dates and other relevant data. Educator Mark Naison, who has developed oral history programs for students in New York, describes his experience:

> Oral History Programs are one of the best antidotes to the sense of historical amnesia among the young people we work with. When we tell our students to interview parents, grandparents and neighbors about things that happened in the past, we not only stimulate a dialogue between children and adults that takes place all too rarely in today's society, we honor community story telling traditions that are in danger of dying out. In our immigrant and working class neighborhoods, there are tens of thousands, if not millions of elderly people who were brought up among great story tellers but who have not had a chance to share their wisdom and experience before an appreciative

audience. Having young people sit down and record their stories not only gives the people interviewed an enhanced sense of purpose, it unleashes a creative power that can be a force in its own right. It can give young people doing the interviews a new respect for people they took for granted, and give the entire school community exposure to stories that have the power to uplift, amuse, excite and inspire everyone who hears them.[3]

FAMILY HISTORY

One of the most common forms of intergenerational oral history is family history. Many families have at least one person who is the "family historian" and feels responsible for collecting and preserving family stories, photos, and other documents, information and memorabilia. The collection of family stories and artifacts often includes an intergenerational aspect, such as an aunt connecting with her parents, siblings, cousins, and nephews. This relatively simple format of getting family members to talk to and about each other can be effectively utilized within an oral history project. As with larger, community-based oral histories, family-based projects can amass valuable anecdotal information and historical documents. When properly collated, such materials can find their way into historical societies and other archiving venues.

The main difference between a family history and an intergenerational oral history is the method of preserving and creating access to the stories and collected items. Generally, family histories are shared only with family members. Even if a product such as a book or DVD is created, this is not considered an archival format unless it is made accessible to the public. Still, family histories are important and enriching for all participants and can be very useful for family members,

---

3. Naison, Mark, "Hip Hop and Oral History: Turning Students Into 'Griots For a New Age,'" Fordham University, p. 1.

oral historians, and historians alike. The family—the starting point for each of us—is also a potential starting point for an exceptional intergenerational oral history project.

THE INTERGENERATIONAL APPROACH

"Kids are so busy these days. I'm sure they wouldn't have time for another activity!" "Young people don't care about history. All they're interested in is their iPods and video games." "I wouldn't even know where to find teens let alone know how to talk to them about the project." "Kids aren't as responsible as adults." "Young people just don't have the necessary skills for this kind of project." "Adding teens to the mix will just make everything more complicated and costly."

Do any of these quotes sound familiar? Perhaps one or two of them ran through your mind at some point. There is some truth to some of these statements. It will take time to find and train the right volunteers, regardless of their age, which may impact your budget and time line. Yet, consider the goals of your project. If they include building community or connecting people with their past, adding an intergenerational element will certainly help. This format can appeal to teachers and after-school activity leaders looking for more engaging adventures in learning. Museums and other community centers can utilize this kind of project to augment youth participation, now and in the future. The idea that young people are, well, just too young for this kind of

---

WORKING WITH YOUTH VOLUNTEERS

"This project was open to volunteer interviewers of any age. Initially, the project directors didn't want to take high school students because they thought they wouldn't be as responsible as adults, that they would be less committed and less able to perform the necessary tasks. After working with some high school volunteers, however, they conceded that they had been wrong in thinking students wouldn't be up to the task. The students we had were dynamos!"

—Project Manager, *Life Storytelling Project*

thing is simply untrue. Even elementary school children can appreciate and support the gathering of stories.

Another misconception is that young people are not interested in history or even their own family stories. They may roll their eyes at hearing that story again, yet still value it. They may be very busy but still long for a really interesting project to sink their teeth into. They may be bored at school and need a more engaging activity. They may seem to live in a virtual world while still hungering to learn about this one. Implementing oral history into the classroom will

---

ARE TEENS INTERESTED IN HISTORY?

Interviewer: What would you say to someone who is doing an oral history project who thinks that teens wouldn't be interested?

Interviewee: You must be out of your minds! We had a teacher who was nice person but what we mainly did was read the book and we learned nothing. No one can recall anything from the class. You ask us about anything from the Chinese dynasties and we won't know!

We are happy to have a teacher who can help us understand our own history.... Oral history helps us to remember, understand and connect it with other historical ideas from the present.

History teachers, if you want us to have A's in your class, you will talk to us. History isn't always boring. I thought history was boring but that's because I always had to read books. When I hear it, it becomes so interesting and I want to hear more, do research. A lot of kids are like that.

In the future, when there's president that we have to vote for or people in our generation run for president, at least we will remember American history and other countries' history so we'll know what to do and how not to ruin what we have, so our great dynasty does not fall and crumble. Remembering our history will help us help the majority of our people.

—Youth participant, *youTHink*

TELL ME YOUR STORY—PLEASE!

Youth interviewer 1: I feel like many elders, not just the ones in Chinese community, but in this world as well, are not very willing to share their stories because they thought that the next generation is not interested. Life has advanced so much now that the young people now probably don't bother to hear how they had to do hard work when they were kids, how they had to work in a restaurant. Kids now grow up with game boys and video games, so I just want to let them know that we really are interested. If you like to share your stories, please don't hesitate to tell your grandchildren about it. The probability is that they very interested to learn about it, but that they are afraid to ask you.

Youth interviewer 2: Storytelling is such an important part of every culture and everybody's life. It is something that is lost but needs to be re-found because we are always on cell phones, and always emailing. We lose that face-to-face, person-to-person connection. It would be such an amazing experience for everyone to gather around and just listen to stories for hours. I think it is really important to just share that experience and bring that back the experience.

—Youth participants, *Oakland Chinatown Oral History Project*

almost certainly come as a welcome change from standard curriculum.

Teachers have many requirements to fulfill in the classroom, many of which can be met with a properly designed oral history project. While it may take extra effort to create an oral history project, there may be volunteers, grants or support within the school to make it happen. For those outside the classroom, allowing youth to volunteer will attract those who are really interested and will therefore make the time to participate.

Many young people are earnestly looking for interesting activities and opportunities to meet new people. By welcoming them and getting them engaged in your project, you have the opportunity not only to pass on important skills but also help build their self-esteem.

BENEFITS TO ELDERS

One of the greatest challenges facing elders today is a sense of isolation and futility. Whether they are living alone at home or within a care-giving environment, there is a real danger of losing touch with the world and the ability to experience fulfillment and meaning. The practice of life storytelling, or reminiscing, is a scientifically proven method for improving elders' quality of life.[4] Reminiscence serves a number of functions, including promoting self-understanding, transcending physical limitations, increasing self worth, alleviating depression, and helping people deal with crises, loss, and life transitions.[5] In fact, the act of bringing positive memories into the present has even been shown to contribute a resistance to disease,[6] including dementia and Alzheimer's disease.[7]

Organizations that utilize storytelling therapies also report many benefits to the storyteller's family and even their own care-giving staff. By learning about the elder's life and achievements, they can draw links between present behavior and past experiences. Caregivers gain a better understanding and respect for the person they are caring for and can find more ways to connect with them and even learn from them. By participating in an intergenerational oral history project, the elder has the opportunity to not only experience life review but also contribute to a larger pursuit and engage with young people—a gift that is becoming all too rare.

---

4. Butler, R. N., "The life review: An unrecognized bonanza," *International Journal of Aging and Human Development,* v.12, pp. 35-38, 1980.
5. Jones, E, "Reminiscence Therapy for older women with depression: effects of nursing intervention classification in assisted-living long-term care," *Journal for Gerontological Nursing,* Vol. 29, no. 7, p. 27, 2003.
6. Stride Magazine online, 2001, http://www.stridemagazine.com/articles/2001/q4/reminiscing/.
7. "Dementia Care Practice Recommendations for Assisted Living Residences and Nursing Homes," Alzheimer's Association, 2006.

VALUE TO ELDERS

"Some of the benefits we've seen from our program are:

- **Validation of the person.** [Sharing life stories and wisdom] gives credence to what they feel, believe and have accomplished. 'Hey—I really did do something good. That's more than I thought I had to say.'
- **Culture change.** In most traditional nursing homes, it's based on routines and preferences of the staff and institution versus resident directed care. We need to know what's important to the residents, so these stories are a vehicle for that.
- **Life goes on.** So many people coming into our community see this as a dead end, the last place they will go. This helps them see this may be their last physical home but not the end of their lives.
- **Real impact on nurturing relationships** between members of the community. Someone in the kitchen reads a story and discovers they used to live on the same street in the same small town as one of the residents. It becomes less about 'I'm here to do a job' and more about 'I'm forming a relationship because you are now a person to me.'
- **Bond between residents and volunteers.** When the story ends, that connection remains. Many times, after the story ends, they continue to spend time together, send a birthday card, come to visit. 50-60% maintain some sort of communication.
- **Making dreams come true.** Our activities director is working with a resident having her 101st birthday. She went to her life story and learned that [the resident] loves birds and has never seen a bald eagle, so she contacted an agency and they are bringing in a live bald eagle. She can continue to experience things she's always wanted to experience.

This is another way of connecting and building community, which is what it's all about."

—Project Manager, *Life Storytelling Program*

There's no better way to teach people, young or old, than with hands-on experience. Young people bring vibrancy and wisdom that can add value to your project and its ramifications for your community and beyond. Elders and young people thrive when they are allowed to contribute. When they are interested and given the opportunity, young people can provide enormous support and their enthusiasm can act as fuel for the rest of your team. Bringing generations together to share stories bolsters legacy. By adding an intergenerational element to your project, everyone wins.

VALUE TO YOUTH

"To young people, it's not boring. It's not going to be another history assignment where you connect the dots and write an essay about the past. You are actually interacting with your family and being able to know and understand who you are.... You will be able to remember and awaken your ancestral past and the indigenous background your family holds. We as Latinos and we as Africans and we as the minorities really need to remember who we are, because our past, our culture, the food we eat, is what shapes us and we can't forget that and walk the future blinded. We have to know who we are, and accept it. And it's very interesting, very interesting. You learn a lot.

"It was really fun. Also, being recorded for the project makes you feel pretty cool. The whole process—talking to your peers, hearing stories from other kids and other schools—builds connections and brings us closer together. Just because we're different, some of us have bigger eyes or darker skin, but we are all people and we all have stories and we all have to have respect for each other, regardless of our backgrounds."

—Youth participant, *youTHink*

CHAPTER TWO

Project Overview

Why was Solomon recognized as the wisest man in the world? Because he knew more stories (proverbs) than anyone else. Scratch the surface in a typical boardroom and we're all just cavemen with briefcases, hungry for a wise person to tell us stories.

—Alan Kay, computer scientist

Now that you've decided to instigate an intergenerational oral history project, what do you *do*? This overview of the oral history process can help you grasp the totality of a standard oral history project as well as distinguish some of its basic components. As you will see, each of these steps is essential and leads naturally to the other. The diagram on the following page illustrates the basic structure of the oral history process, each step of which will be discussed in detail in the following chapters.

PREPARATION

Every successful project begins with great preparation. Like a redwood tree, a successful project needs a sturdy root system to keep it grounded, a base from which it can soar. In the case of an intergenerational oral history project, your preparation will include three major components.

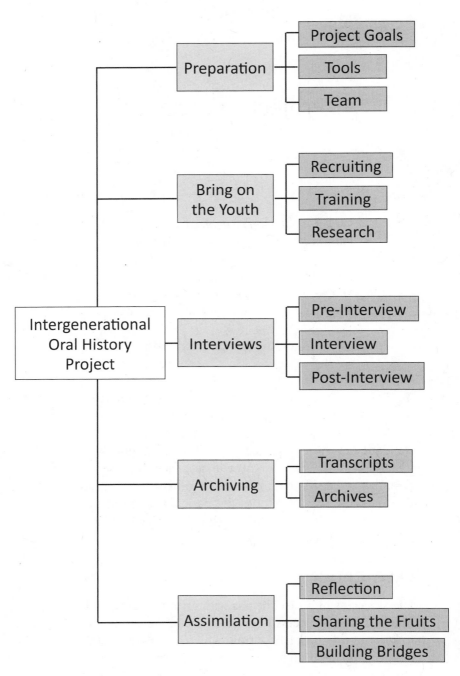

Figure 2: Project Overview

Project Goals: As a wise man once said, how can you know where you're going if you don't know where you're starting from? This essential step includes defining and refining the overall goals for your project and how these goals will be reached. What are you trying to achieve, and what steps will you take to achieve them? The main thing here is to be specific as possible, so you can see when you've met your goals and assess if you are going off track. This goal statement is arguably the most important document you will create: this is the blueprint for the entire project.

Tools: What items will you need in order to manifest your goals? Your tools include documents, such as a project budget, as well as equipment, such as a recording device.

Your Team: Who do you need on your team to make this project a success? What skills do you have, and what skills are needed? Will you be hiring people or working with volunteers? Your team includes project staff, the people you will be interviewing, and others who will be supporting the project, such as archivists and community advisors.

BRING ON THE YOUTH

Now that the groundwork is laid, it's time to incorporate your team of young people into the project. Depending on the nature and goals of your project, you can include young people in almost any capacity, from interviewers to advisors to general project support.

Recruiting: Schools and malls may be full of them, but how can you get young people engaged with your project? In this section you'll find "hooks" to interest young people in your project as well as pointers to help you successfully convey your ideas to a young audience.

Training: You want your project to be a success, and you want the young people to feel successful as interviewers. So, it's time for some training. The training period not only prepares the young people for their role as interviewers; it also deepens the bonds between the project teammates. Moreover, it gives you the opportunity to assess the skills and motivation of your team members, therefore helping you make the right decisions in moving the project forward.

Research: Some amount of research is critical in a project of this nature. By doing research of historical data relevant to the interviews, the youth gain confidence, which in turn helps them ask appropriate interview questions and make connections to their own experiences. Your research can take many forms—and can be a lot of fun.

INTERVIEWS

Some oral history interviews are very simple: you think of a question, which you ask of any passersby. Other interviews, though, have a specific purpose and therefore need to be thought through more completely. With intergenerational interviews, especially when the interviewers have little experience, it's prudent to set them up for success by implementing an extended interview process.

Pre-interview meeting and prep: One important attribute of a successful interview is good rapport between interviewer and interviewee. This rapport is easier to achieve when the interviewer and interviewee have met before the actual interview. The pre-interview meeting is a time to meet informally and obtain the information you need to refine your interview questions and set up your interview space.

Conducting the Interview: Here we go! Now that all the pieces are in place, what actually happens when the interviewer and interviewee sit across from each other? This section describes what a successful interview looks like, and provides many pointers for how can you bring it about.

Post-interview: Now that the interview is finished, what else do you need before everyone leaves the room? This is also a key time to organize your content and therefore set yourself up for an easeful next step.

ARCHIVING

You've done it—the interviews are complete. That means your project is complete, right? Not really. Now that the interviews are recorded, it's time to format the interview content to ensure your hard work is preserved and accessible to others.

Transcripts: The most widely accepted form of oral history documentation is the transcript, which is a written copy of your recording. Transcribing can be very time-consuming to create so it's helpful to know up front what will be required and what your other options are.

Archiving: Once the transcripts are complete, chances are strong you have accumulated quite a bit of material. The next step is to consider how and where you will store the materials so they are safe and accessible.

ASSIMILATION

What a feeling—the interviews are complete and are safely archived. Now it's time to assimilate, celebrate, and share what you've learned. This section provides ideas for final projects, ways to share your findings with the public, and tips for wrapping up all the details.

Reflection: Oral histories involve a lot of busy work. In addition to focusing on the details, however, it's also extremely worthwhile to spend time reflecting on lessons learned. The impact of the oral history experience can often be very deep. Participants experience emotions and gain new skills and knowledge that can be revelatory. Take advantage of this opportunity to integrate the emotional impact and learning lessons so that participants make the most of their contribution and experience.

Project Finale: One rewarding aspect of oral history is sharing your findings with a larger community. This can be especially rewarding for young people and often gives them an extra incentive for their participation. Some ideas for assimilating and sharing your project include writing and art projects, public events, and exhibitions.

Building Bridges: Chances are, you have met many people as a result of this project. Perhaps you have come across similar projects, or have generated new ideas for your next project. Before you move on, this is a great time to acknowledge the connections you've made and look at how you may want to develop them further.

ORAL HISTORY TIME LINE: PRE-INTERVIEW

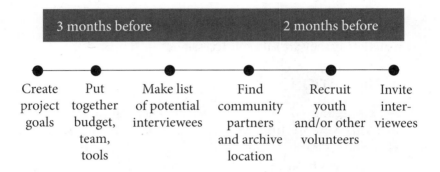

ORAL HISTORY TIME LINE: POST-INTERVIEW

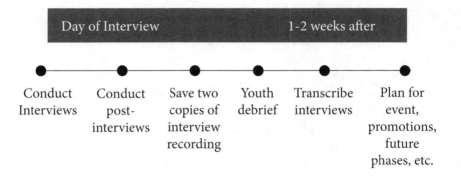

Figure 3: Sample Oral History Project Timelines

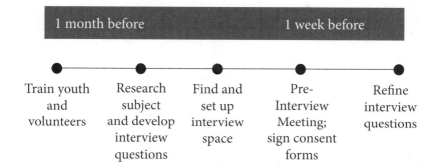

1 month before			1 week before	
Train youth and volunteers	Research subject and develop interview questions	Find and set up interview space	Pre-Interview Meeting; sign consent forms	Refine interview questions

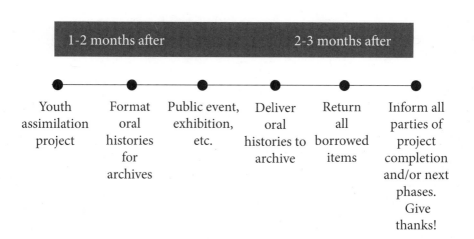

1-2 months after			2-3 months after		
Youth assimilation project	Format oral histories for archives	Public event, exhibition, etc.	Deliver oral histories to archive	Return all borrowed items	Inform all parties of project completion and/or next phases. Give thanks!

Wrap up and Celebrate: With a project of this nature, there are inevitably many details to wrap up, many of which are highlighted here. Then, when it's all said and done, you definitely have something to celebrate: a contribution to history that will benefit all who come in contact with it, for generations to come.

CHAPTER THREE

Preparation

Stories are bridges from one mind to another.

—Martha Holloway

You don't build a bridge by just throwing any old thing across a ravine. Rather, you do some groundwork first: find the right materials, the right place for the bridge, the right people to build it. The same is true for building story bridges.

The best way to set yourself up for success is to come prepared. The better prepared you are, the better you can act efficiently, assess your progress, and manage the unexpected circumstances that are sure to arise. Preparation includes three areas that need to be addressed at the onset of your project: creating project goals, acquiring the necessary tools, and putting together your team. The most important step of your preparation is the articulation of your goals.

PROJECT GOALS

In envisioning an oral history project, most people focus on the interviews. This is the fun part, after all. Yet in order to ensure the success of your project, and even your interviews, it's vital to ask: **What are you trying to achieve with this project?** Think about who you are trying to serve and why. If you are applying for or utilizing a grant, be sure to consider the grant deliverables as you set your goals. Be specific and realistic, but don't be afraid to aim high.

To articulate the project goals, gather your core team together and discuss what it is you are trying to achieve, and why. Don't worry about language at this point; just collect thoughts. Once you've decided on the central purpose, choose someone to craft those thoughts into a clear, succinct mission statement.[8] Mission statements are at most three sentences or one paragraph long; a vision statement would be longer and include more details. This statement can then be sent to the entire team for edits. Be prepared to tinker over language. This document is the blueprint for your entire project and sets the intention for how you will proceed. It's like setting the course for a ship: very important if you want to avoid ramming into icebergs. Continue to refer back to this document throughout the course of the project so you can assess if you are staying on track.

PROJECT GOALS

"When creating their goals, the Oakland Chinatown Oral History Project [OCOHP] team considered the bigger picture. In addition to collecting stories, they wanted to address the shift in family structures within the Asian-American community. Ties between generations were being broken, especially between youth and elders.

To address this challenge, the goals of the OCOHP included not only the collection and preservation of stories but also the strengthening of intergenerational bonds. This was what drove the team to instigate an *intergenerational* oral history project."

—Project Director, *Oakland Chinatown Oral History Project*

Once your goals are set, it is time to address how you will achieve them. Again, be specific about your strategies. This is also the time to be very practical. For example, if you have a small budget, you probably won't be able to produce an

---

8. See Appendix 1 for sample Mission Statements

STEPS TO CREATING PROJECT GOALS

- Ask, "What are we trying to achieve with this project?"
- Ask, "Why is this important?"
- Be specific and aim high.
- Craft answers into a mission statement.
- Ask, "How will we achieve these goals?"
- Be specific and realistic.

hour-long documentary for PBS. Ensure the language is clear enough for someone outside the project team to understand as you may use this document to apply for grants or educate volunteers or the media about your project.

TOOLS

With your mission statement complete, you are now ready to assemble the tools you'll need to carry out the project. Tools include the budget document, consent forms and equipment.

Budget Document

Before you run out and buy a new video camera, it is critical to address one of the most common challenges of oral history projects: the budget.[9] Take some time to figure out exactly how much money you have and how you will allocate it. Instead of buying that camera, you may have to borrow one, which is just fine—more on this later. In formulating your budget, think through the various stages of your project. Your budget may include: staff (such as a project manager, video editor, or transcriptionist); equipment (such as cameras, recorders, microphones, or an external hard drive); research materials (such as books, museum tickets, or honorarium for a guest lecturer); supplies (anything from paper and pens, to display materials, to snacks for an event); printing; postage; transportation; and promotions.

---

9. See Appendix 2 for sample Budget Document

IDEAS FOR WORKING WITH A SMALL BUDGET

- Borrow equipment instead of purchasing
- Build a team of volunteers or interns
- Utilize free conference call services
- Find community partners and vendors to donate space, services (such as printing) or products (such as refreshments for your event).
- Look online for free transcription software and website templates
- Utilize web 2.0 interfaces, such as Google docs, to facilitate the sharing of documents and decrease printing expenses

Consent Forms

A consent form, also called a release form, is a legal document that verifies each party's informed consent to having their interview recorded, preserved and made accessible. All interviewees and interviewers must sign this form. It's important to note—and explain to the interviewee—that in signing a consent form, the interviewee is not signing away their rights to their story. They are merely indicating their agreement that this particular interview be collected and utilized within the project parameters.

Consent forms must include four items:

1. **Who you are:** Name of sponsoring institution and/or project
2. **What you will get** from the person signing the form: interviews, photos, etc.
3. **Why you are getting** these items: for a project, publication, website, etc.
4. **What you will do** with the items: put them in a library, give the signee a copy, etc.

These four points constitute informed consent and must be present in a written and signed document. Other related topics, such as copyright, are optional and will be discussed in Chapter Six.

If you plan to take photos or videos of project participants to post on your website or in an exhibit or other public forum, include the use of images in the release form. Similarly, if you are borrowing objects or photographs for use in an exhibition or event, you will want to provide their owners with an acquired object form that clearly states their intention to loan the object for your purposes. Young people under the age of eighteen must have their parents co-sign any legal forms, such as consent forms and photo release forms.[10]

Equipment

Equipment needs vary widely from project to project. Here are the basics for any recording of oral histories:

- Audio recording device, preferably with external microphone(s)
- Computer
- Camera
- Extra batteries, extension cords, memory cards, etc.

That's it! That's all you really need to record stories and store the files. I recommend a camera so you can take photos of the interviewees and "action shots" of your process. Of course you could spend thousands of dollars on recording equipment, which you may need if you are making a high-quality recording for the radio or TV. For most projects, however, you don't necessarily need a fancy recorder or camera. Most new computers these days come with a microphone and camera. If you plan to share the audio interviews on your website, by podcast, or even burn to a CD, an inexpensive digital audio recorder may suffice.

Audio Recorders

Keep in mind that **your audio recording device is your most important piece of equipment**. It doesn't have to be expensive, but it must be good quality. It's worth your time to research the best audio recorder for your needs before running out and buying the cheapest or most expensive

---

10. Consent and Release Form, Appendix 3; Consent Form for Minors, Appendix 4; Acquired Objects Form, Appendix 5

model.[11] Consider also the longevity of your project and what equipment you might need for future phases. You might be better off investing in great equipment rather than having to replace or repair your equipment every year.

External microphones, when used properly, increase the sound quality of any recording. Decent microphones can be found for as little as $40 and can make a huge difference in recording quality and therefore how the recording can be utilized. Without a good mic, even the best recorder may not provide the quality you need. If you just don't have the funds for microphones, be sure to conduct your interviews in a quiet space and keep the recording device near the interviewer and interviewee.

DIGITAL AUDIO RECORDING FORMATS

Digital audio formats will undoubtedly continue to change over the years. At this moment in our technological history, the most common digital audio formats are WAV and MP3 files.

WAV files are higher quality and therefore create larger files. You always want to record at the highest quality, which means recording in a WAV format. Later, you can convert these WAV files into other formats that suit your needs.

Websites and MP3 players need smaller files, such as MP3 files. The general rule is to use WAV files to record and MP3 files to deliver.

Video Recorders

Video footage is priceless. Like audio recordings, video footage captures the many nuances of the interview and is an excellent medium for sharing stories at events, exhibits, on the web, and beyond. In addition, video captures facial expressions, hand gestures and other non-verbal communication. Seeing the interviewee can help people connect more readily to what

---

11. The website www.oralhistory.org/technology is a good resource for equipment research and is updated frequently.

To Record or Not To Record

This is one of the most important questions to address before getting too deep into your project as the answer to this question will greatly impact the direction, logistics and longevity of your project. Some people choose not to record the interviews because they don't want to deal with recording equipment or they are afraid that having a recorder will make the interviewees nervous. Without question, though, **recording of interviews is highly recommended for any story-collecting endeavor.**

First of all, by its very definition, an oral history needs to be recorded. An unrecorded conversation can be interesting and useful, but it is not a primary source. Secondly, recordings capture not only every word that is spoken verbatim but also the voices, accents, pauses, and other nuances that written documents cannot replicate. Thirdly, it is far more efficient and effective to record an interview than to try to retain and capture all the information by memory alone. Most importantly, a recording will help ensure that the words and stories with all their important nuances will be available for posterity.

In other words, even if you don't know what you'll do with the recordings, make them anyway.

they are saying. It's always a good idea to video the interviews even if you don't yet know how you'll use the videos or have the budget to edit them; you may find a volunteer editor down the line.

If you decide to film your interviews, you may not need an expensive video camera. Most interviews run about forty-five minutes to an hour so you'll need enough memory to record for lengthy periods, ideally without stopping to change batteries or tapes. You'll definitely want a tripod for the camera so you are assured a clean, unmoving shot.

These days you can find handheld video cameras that are very easy to use and download for less than $100. If you want to share videos on the web, this is all you need. To create videos for TV, you will need a better camera. You'll also need someone who knows how to use it. As with the rest of your equipment, consider borrowing if you don't have the budget to buy.

Some potential resources for borrowing recording equipment are:

- Project participants and advisors
- Family members
- Schools, especially film or radio classes
- Local cable or radio stations
- IT departments

BORROWING EQUIPMENT

"The library doesn't have a video camera so we borrowed video equipment from the city's IT department. When we told them about our project and our equipment needs, they offered us their camera with mic and tripod. They even came and showed us how to use it!

"Later, the local cable channel was asking city departments if they had any videos about our town. They found out from the IT department about our project and actually aired our video a few times."

—Project Director, *Fusing Identities*

Archiving Equipment

In addition to recording equipment, consider the equipment you'll need to archive your materials. Hard copies of documents, photos and other print products should be archived in airtight boxes and kept in a dark, cool location. Digital files also need to be archived thoughtfully; saving one copy on your computer's hard drive is a start but, as you'll see in Chapter Six, proper archiving requires more than one storage location.

An excellent way to keep all your digital files together in one safe place is to purchase an external hard drive to be used solely to archive your project materials. This is especially useful if you are creating video files that take up lots of space.

The more extensive your project, the more complex archiving becomes. Densho, the non-profit organization that oversees the Japanese American Legacy Project, has an entire room of high-tech archiving equipment and a full-time staff person dedicated to maintaining their digital archives.

Be it a room of equipment, a dedicated external hard drive, or just a few CDs, your archiving equipment is essential for the survival of your valuable collection.

YOUR TEAM

Whether you are a teacher, librarian, oral history expert, or student, you will probably need some help with your project. Depending on the project's complexity and your resources, you can consider hiring full- or part-time staff or work with volunteers; most projects use some combination. There are pros and cons to both hiring staff and working with volunteers. For example, hiring someone may be expensive but may also help you get the job done better and quicker. Or, depending on your project goals, you may choose to use volunteers for certain tasks so they can be exposed to new skills.

Your core team will consist of a project director and/ or manager, interviewers, and interviewees. Some projects function very well with a small team, while others benefit from a larger pool of support staff and volunteers. Here are the basic skill sets that many oral history projects utilize:

- Interviewer(s)
- Oral history expert: Train volunteers, oversee interview and archiving processes
- Project Manager: Oversee time line and deliverables
- Historian: Provide historical information, context and sources; suggest research methodologies and framework for historical research
- Grant writer
- Community liaison: Build and maintain connections with community partners and advisors; participate in community-building strategies and events

- Transcriptionist
- Archivist
- Administrative support: Organize paperwork; set up meetings; write grants and promotional copy; provide support as needed
- Public relations: Formulate and implement promotional strategies; outreach to media and social networks; send and follow up on press releases and Public Service Announcements; oversee marketing collateral design and production
- Event planner
- Exhibit Curator
- Audio and/or video editor
- Fundraising specialist
- Media, Web and/or Social networking specialists

Finding Interviewees

No interview can take place without the interviewer and interviewee. We'll talk about interviewers in the next chapter. How do you find and select the right interviewees, specifically in the elder population?

In addition to local neighborhoods, groups of elders can be found in senior centers, retirement communities, veteran events, and religious institutions, amongst other places. Because of the many benefits to their constituents, many senior centers and communities are eager to connect with youth groups. They may also be able to recommend individuals or groups with specific backgrounds and knowledge. You can also contact local clubs or community service groups, such as the Elks Club.

While looking out in the community, look also closer to home. Do any of the project participants or advisors have acquaintances who meet your qualifications? Who can they recommend? Consider local businesspeople and their families. Ask for recommendations without making any promises—you will want to vet every potential interviewee to make sure you end up with a group that can help you achieve the full spectrum of your project goals. Finally, the interviewers' own families can often be an ideal place to find interviewees, especially for projects whose goals include the deepening of family connections.

Selecting Interviewees

Whether you have a group of interviewees ready to go or you have no idea yet who to interview, the same criteria apply. **The ideal interviewee is willing and able to be interviewed and has the information you are looking for.** This may sound obvious, but it can sometimes be an effort to find people who meet both of these criteria. In addition, take some time to specify other characteristics of your ideal narrator. For example, you may want to focus on people of a certain age, from a certain place, who have witnessed a specific event.

Often times, people who want to be interviewed are "good talkers." They might even be known in their community for their storytelling. The most eager interviewees, however, are not always the best interviewees. For example, one project director signed up an interviewee based on a great story he'd heard her tell at a community meeting. When the same woman was being interviewed, however, she constantly veered off topic and repeated the same story several times. He expected her to be his best interview—after all, her storytelling prowess had made her locally famous—yet her behavior changed dramatically within the very different atmosphere of an interview. This is not always the case, of course, but keep your eye on the quiet ones as well as the most loquacious.

What about the person you want to interview that just isn't interested? Common responses to an interview request are: "I don't have anything to talk about. My life has not been special or interesting," "My English is not good enough," or simply, "I don't want to talk about it." Sometimes people say these things because they are not used to being the focus of attention. They may really believe they have nothing of interest to say. This is particularly true of older women, especially those who never worked outside the home and think they haven't participated in events of "historical importance." Sometimes persistence is the best answer, gently convincing your prospect that you really do care about and respect their experience. Other people just will never feel comfortable being interviewed and it's best to let them be.

For people whose native tongue is different from the language of the interview, it's very common to feel uncomfortable being interviewed and especially being recorded. They may feel ashamed of their language skills and potential grammatical mistakes. It can be helpful to let them know that others in the same position have agreed and enjoyed the experience. Have a community member they respect make the invitation and describe the benefits of their participation. Sometimes, though, this may not be enough. Some people may want the option to correct their errors on the interview transcripts. Consider ways you can make interviewees comfortable without complicating or diluting your own process.

Language is not the only potential barrier. Some people are very happy talking but just don't want to talk about what you want them to talk about. When confronted with this situation, think about the reasons why they may not want to talk about it. Many elders grew up in an environment very different from today, when people simply did not speak about their personal lives and secrets were kept forever. Many subjects that interest us today were taboo in their day. If they do agree to speak with you, keep in mind that you may be the very first person they have ever opened up to in this way. Moreover, you are asking them not only to talk to you but to be recorded, their words forever public and "out of their control." Show them that you respect their experiences whether they'll talk to you or not. Show them, when applicable, that others in a similar situation have agreed to be interviewed. Have a friend or respected community member ask on your behalf. Offer to mow their lawn! Sometimes young people can be more effective in coaxing elders to open up by showing their interest or talking about why these stories matter to them. Be understanding, persistent, patient, and honest. If they still say no, give them your contact info and move on.

Building a community team

In addition to interviewers and interviewees, it can be very helpful to build a team of community members to act as an advisory committee and help shepherd your project along. Such a team can increase community involvement, give you access to greater resources, and provide clarity and direction. Community members can contribute their skills and contacts, spread the word about the project, recommend interviewees and sometimes even coax them to participate. Picking the right team members can also give your project legitimacy in the community, so think strategically. Consider including young people on your advisory team. Their ideas and enthusiasm can be very helpful in moving the project in exciting directions and getting other young people involved.

While it does take some effort to keep such a group informed and involved, a well-managed advisory team can provide immense support, motivation and resources that make it well worth your time. One key to success is designating one person to be in charge of managing the committee. This way, all communications to the advisory team go through one person only. Clear communication breeds greater harmony between team players, making it easier and more fun for everyone to achieve their goals.

Community support can come from institutions as well as individuals. Many museums, libraries, historical societies and other institutions are deeply invested in creating legacy and building community. On a practical level, creating partnerships with other institutions, such as community centers joining forces or a library collaborating with a school, can double the potential resources and exponentially expand the outreach of your project. Word of mouth is still the best way to encourage participation, so the more mouths talking about your project, the better.

In addition to documentation, the oral history process also addresses one of the greatest challenges faced by communities: divisions between community members. Like everyone else, institutions are affected by the growing

POTENTIAL COMMUNITY COLLABORATORS

- Museums
- Libraries
- Schools or specific classes
- Historical Societies
- Media outlets (such as local cable or radio stations)
- Community organizations
- Youth groups
- Religious institutions
- Community centers
- Cultural centers
- Service clubs
- Chamber of Commerce
- Universities
- City Advisors
- Senior centers or communities

divide between individuals of different generations, races, and other groups. The oral history process can ameliorate this division by giving participants the opportunity not only for sharing stories but also for reflection. Reflection during and after the story sharing helps participating individuals find commonality, gain understanding and accept their differences. Our American society is becoming more and more segmented. How do you bridge that gap? One way is sharing stories.

Sustaining a successful collaboration

It's often easier to create than to sustain a partnership. At the beginning, everyone is excited and eager to get involved. Once all the balls are in the air, however, things can get somewhat complicated. Here are some tips to sustaining a successful collaboration:

- Ensure that the personnel from each participating institution really understand the project and partnership and are committed to this process and making it a success. Representatives from each party need to have a good working relationship. A partnership may look great on paper but that's not enough—the people have to work well together.

- Any successful collaboration has to be a win-win for all the institutions involved. Each party's needs and skills should complement each other. For example, a project looking for a permanent archive would do well to partner with a library that wants more oral histories in their collection. This is a really good fit.

DREAM TEAM

"The Oakland Chinatown Oral History Project has had community collaborators throughout all phases of the project. This helped us meet our goals on our very limited budget. The second phase revolved around capturing more stories that we wanted to share with a larger audience. We contacted StoryCorps, who was in the Bay Area at the time, and discovered that they wanted more Asian-American stories in their collection. We arranged for them to come out to our center and offer a full day of recording, including personnel and equipment. We both did the promoting and it was extremely successful.

"For the third phase, we partnered with a radio broadcasting class at a local college. Every semester, the students in that class produce radio stories that are eventually broadcasted on a local radio station. They needed stories, and we needed historical research and more media outreach. The students are doing historical research about the part of our community that was greatly affected by urban development— just the research we needed for Phase Three. And they get to use our interview content from Phase Three. This was the right match for all of us.

"Before this phase, we met with ten to twelve professors at the college who were all interested in collaborating. We were very thoughtful about collaborating with the class that made the most sense for our project."

—Project Director, *Oakland Chinatown Oral History Project*

- Make sure everyone understands their role and responsibilities. This way, nothing falls through the cracks and you can proceed with the greatest efficiency.
- Take the time to build trust. Don't assume that the trust is there. Trust blossoms when each party is doing their part and progress is being made.
- Keep all parties up to date. Without inundating your partners with needless information or cheerleading, be sure to share your successes as well as any challenges that are effecting your time line or productivity.
- Expect things to take longer than you think they're going to take.
- Always attempt to communicate clearly. Don't take it for granted that communication will be clear. Do your part by reviewing action items, time lines, and other pertinent information at the end of each meeting.
- Make time for periodic face-to-face meetings.
- Include a social component, such as combining lunch with a meeting, to give people a chance to get to know each other as well as contribute to the project.

BEGIN AT THE END

It may seem early, but the beginning of your project is the right time to think about how and where your work will end up. Specifically, now is the time to think about how you will be archiving your recordings and whatever other products are created alongside them. While archiving is often an afterthought for community-based oral histories, some would argue that an unarchived oral history project isn't even worth the time. In fact, the step of archiving is what makes oral history different from other means of sharing stories.

The best time to form a partnership with an archivist or archiving institution is the very beginning of your project. If you are hoping or planning to place your oral history in a library, it's best to visit the library and speak to a librarian about what their requirements are before you get started. For example, they may require a specific consent form to be signed by all interviewees, which is much harder to do at the end of a project. See Chapter 7 for an in-depth discussion of the benefits of archiving, as well as information about how to go about it.

With your project goals, core team and tools in place, you have constructed a solid foundation. You are ready to expand your team and take the next step. It's time to bring on the youth!

LESSONS LEARNED: PREPARATION

Wish we had...

- Been more mindful about the entire process when putting together our budget. By the time we got to transcribing, we were out of funds.
- Bought better recorders! We bought a whole bunch of cheap recorders so the students could take them with them for the duration of the project and we'd have plenty for next year. Unfortunately, many of them broke, the recordings didn't come out very well, and now we'll have to go out and buy more. This time we'll go for quality over quantity!
- Modified our project goals after getting a grant. Instead of working towards the grant requirements the whole time, we ended up doing a lot of last minute scrambling.
- A dedicated team member to help welcome and orient the volunteers. We spent all this time recruiting but didn't do as well with the follow up.

So glad we...

- Talked to and ended up teaming up with a local museum. We didn't think they'd give us the time of day but as it turned out, they were thrilled to work with us and provided a lot of support, including space and a well-oiled promotional process and network.
- Carefully selected the interviewees. We had a lot of volunteers but made sure we only chose the ones who met all of our criteria.
- Brought in an oral history expert. We thought we could manage the whole project even though no one on our team had any oral history experience. We waited until total overwhelm then finally hired someone who ended up saving us so much time and money. Should have done that from the start!

CHAPTER FOUR

Bring On the Youth

I will open my mouth in a parable
I will utter dark sayings of old.
Things that we have heard and known,
that our fathers told us.
We will not hide them from their children,
but tell it to the coming generations.

—Bible, Psalm 78:1-4

You want to bring young people onto your team because you believe they will benefit your project and the project will benefit them. Depending on your time line and goals, young people can participate in every part of an oral history project, from management to interviewing, transcribing to event planning. Once they are on your team, you can assess their skills and level of commitment and design their participation accordingly. First, though, you need to get young people involved. Then, with the right training and tools, they will stay involved.

RECRUITING

The greatest obstacle people mention when considering an intergenerational project is that they don't know where to find young people to participate. The simplest answer is to go where the young people are: the schools. Inside the classroom, you can meet necessary education standards by integrating an oral history project into your curriculum.[12]

Outside the classroom, your project may help students meet their school's community service requirement. They may be able to gain extra credit, or their participation can shore up their college application. High school seniors and college students may be interested in an internship position. You can speak directly to teachers and find out who their best history students are. Ask them to suggest young people who are interested in what you have to offer, such as interviewing skills, editing film, or building a website. Many young people —maybe more than you think—are very interested in hearing stories from the past. They may just need someone to create the opportunity.

In addition to schools, after-school programs present another venue to find young people. Community centers, youth groups, service clubs, libraries, churches, museums and other places that offer youth programs may be interested in collaborating or promoting your project. Many projects are initiated in such places, where they already have a core group of young people who regularly attend. As Glenn Whitman, author

RECRUITMENT SUCCESS

"We have a lot of young people who come to our center all the time so we thought we'd have no problem getting volunteers. Still, months went by and only a few people signed up. We made some recruitment flyers and put them up in the center and around town, and we put an ad in a few local papers. Once the ads were placed, we got lots of interest. In the end, about 90% of our youth volunteers came from these recruitment flyers and ads. Sometimes the young people weren't the ones to see the flyer and it still got them here. One mother saw the ad in a local paper. She told her son about it, and he came with a few of his friends."
—Project Manager, *Oakland Chinatown Oral History Project*

---

12. For detailed information, see Glenn Whitman's *Dialogue with the Past*, Altamira Press, 2004.

of *Dialogue with the Past*, suggests, "Museums, community centers and local historical societies should embrace the idea of linking up with the classroom. This gives them an army of people to do the work. It also exposes kids to museums and groups as future members." This kind of collaboration also increases community awareness of your program and can add to new dimensions to your project, now and in the future.

Once you've located where the young people are, don't be shy about promoting your project: hang flyers around town and put ads in local papers.

In addition to print promotions, consider putting on a recruitment event in classes and local youth centers.[13] When recruiting young people, the rule of thumb is to have young people participate in the recruiting. Teens are much more likely to be interested in a program if they see that other teens already value it. Share your plans for the end product, particularly if it includes a public forum such as a radio show, public event, or website.

Find out what aspects of your project are most like to interest your young audience, such as technology, history, travel, and whatever perks may come with the job. Describe some of the places they'll be going and people they'll be meeting. These connections can open a lot of doors for them in the community in addition to opening their minds. Let them know all about it.

OPENING DOORS

"I really enjoyed meeting all these new friends, including the elders who have so many good stories to share. Normally I would not be walking inside City Hall to meet the Vice Mayor of Oakland. What kind of organization would allow you to do that, not to even mention the amount of information I've learned from this? Also, it gives me a lot of new perspectives and things to think about."
—Youth interviewer, *Oakland Chinatown Oral History Project*

---

13. See Appendix 6 for sample Recruitment Event Schedule

Before your recruitment event ends, collect names and contact information of all who show interest. Follow up with a phone call and email within the next few days. Many young people have packed schedules and lots of options but they will make time for your project if they're interested.

What to look for in a volunteer

The most important quality of a volunteer is that they are sincerely interested in the project. It may be the topic, or maybe it's the technology. Whatever the reason, their interest is what will motivate them to stay involved. In addition, you want to look for interviewers who are:

- Good listeners
- Comfortable around elders
- Nonjudgmental: Able to listen and accept viewpoints that are different from one's own. An interview is not a venue for debate. The moment the interviewer becomes judgmental, trust is broken and a door is closed.
- Unshockable: Depending on the interview topic and personality of the interviewee, volunteers may hear stories or witness emotions that can be surprising and powerful. While it's important to be sensitive, you want a team of volunteers who can stay in the moment and get the job done.
- Flexible: Schedules change, plans change, agendas change. This is the nature of intergenerational projects, and you want a team that can go with the flow.
- Responsible: Once the plan is in motion, you want to know that the players will all do their part. This means showing up on time, completing the agreed tasks, and working well with others on the team.
- Interested beyond themselves: Many volunteers will come forward because they have something they want to achieve or gain from the project, such as extra credit or a new skill. That's great—as long as their attitude isn't "all about me." The more invested they are in the overall project goals, the more actively they will support the process.

RECRUITING VOLUNTEERS

"Most of the teens that volunteered for the project were already interested in history to begin with. They liked hearing what life was like, what the buildings were like and the context of this area. Many of the teens were politically motivated. They had just experienced 9/11 and could make connections with other war times.

"And don't underestimate how much they value the adults in their lives! They all said that what they loved the most was talking to their parents about growing up in another country or culture. It's their family, but they want to have a deeper connection—"My parents were younger once; they were like me." Telling the stories makes everything more real to them.

"The hardest part was recruiting adults! We put ads in the paper, flyers in the library, talked to people we knew from library whose relatives were older, and other people brought adults in. It would have been better to have a core group of seniors—better to work with a senior center."

—Project Director, *Fusing Identities*

Working with Minors

When working with minors—children under the age of eighteen—there are legal issues to be aware of. If you will be transporting the youth, you may need special auto insurance as well as a qualified driver. Some equipment, such as heavy or sharp objects, may not be appropriate for use, especially by young children. Most importantly for oral history projects, young people under the age of eighteen must have their parents or legal guardian co-sign any legal forms, such as consent forms and photo releases.[14]

TRAINING

You have assembled a group of youth volunteers with different skills who are participating for different reasons. To

---

14. See Appendix 4 for sample Consent Form for Minors

ensure their success and that of your project, some training is in order.[15] First of all, the volunteers need to be educated about your project and what will be expected of them. You may also want to find out what their personal goals are. Most importantly, you will need to offer training in whatever tasks they'll be performing so they feel competent and confident.

ROLE PLAY

"We do role playing before interviews to train kids to get used to different kinds of subjects—open, closed, crying, cold, talkative, going off subject."
—Project Director, *Telling Their Stories: Oral History Archives Project*

In addition to interview training, spend some time practicing with your equipment. Provide or suggest research tools so they can better understand the topics they'll be investigating. If your interviews will address sensitive topics— and almost all do—the youth may need support to process what they are witnessing. Have a frank and open discussion of what may come up in the interviews to prepare the youth for topics or emotions they may not feel readily comfortable with.

For example, in one training session, the youth were asked to write down their biggest fear about interviewing. One young man wrote: "I don't know what I'd do if one of my questions made them cry." His point was a perfect starting point for a frank discussion about emotions and interviews, after which all the volunteers realized the importance and value of respectful probing. Having this conversation helped them feel better prepared for the surprises sure to come as well as demonstrating that their questions and concerns were being taken seriously.

This preparation time will allow you all to get to know each other and begin to bond. It will also educate you about how you can bring out the best in your team.

---

15. See Appendix 7 for a sample Volunteer Training Schedule

BASIC TRAINING

"Before doing any interviews, our volunteers attend a 3-hour training. The project director talks about process and paperwork. Then, myself and another interviewer talk about story collecting and what to ask. We give a few tips on how to interview—give them a framework and let them find what works for them. We remind them, 'It's about them, not you. Don't try to direct the conversation. Residents just want to talk to you.' It's all about being nonjudgmental, not asking leading questions—that's what makes people safe.

"The volunteers interview each other and then write out the other person's story. This is the most beneficial part by giving them a taste of how rewarding and easy it is to do. We show some examples of stories that have been written, and talk about the importance of keeping the voice of the interviewee instead of the volunteer. For example, 'I was scared when I went to join the army,' vs. 'Jim joined the army at a young age.' We want them to let the interviewee speak about whatever is important to them that day, and that's fine. It doesn't have to be linear."

—Project Manager, *Life Storytelling Program*

Different projects require different training. For the Life Storytelling Program, volunteers act more as "story collectors" than interviewers. Their goal is to listen to whatever the narrator wants to say without guiding them in a particular direction, so they need only a basic knowledge of interview techniques. After attending a 3-hour training they are ready to go.

The Telling Their Stories: Oral History Archives Project, on the other hand, is a semester-long immersion in oral history, focusing on subjects who have experienced great trauma in their lives. Over the course of several months, students execute every phase of the process and receive training every step of the way.

Regardless of how much time you have or the experience of your interviewers, it's always wise to do a little interview practice. Pair up your teams and let them feel and discuss what it's like to both ask questions and talk about themselves. Even better, have them do it in front of the rest of your group, then follow up with a critique session that emphasizes both what was done well and that which could be improved.

Finally, take some time to discuss expectations. What do you expect of the volunteers, and what can they expect from you? For example, you may ask that they attend a certain number of sessions, or clarify who will be communicating with the interviewee about scheduling matters.

DISCUSSING EXPECTATIONS

"Our students are with us for a full year and know they are really in it. At the very beginning when they sign up for the youth radio project, we tell them: These are the dates; there are eight sessions; we expect you to be in every session. We lay out the expectations clearly."

—Project Director, *youTHink*

Components of a basic training

- Overview of project
  - Value of oral history
  - Project goals
- Team
  - Introduce key players and those with whom they'll be working and specify their contact person
  - Introduction exercise that lets volunteers begin to get to know each other
- Interview topics and subjects
- Time lines
- Oral History Methodology specific to your project
  - Preparation, Interviews, Archiving, Assimilation
  - How they will be involved with each step
- Equipment training
  - Focus on sound quality and troubleshooting

DEALING WITH TRAUMATIC SUBJECTS

"We've used Shoah materials to prepare. We've also brought in people who are experts with trauma. We do a trauma workshop with the students, a 2-½ hour workshop to help students understand the therapeutic nature of the interview process...so the kids are clear that the person is not being exploited. Repetition of stories is *in most cases* an important part of the interviewee's healing process; this is especially true when the interviewees volunteer to be interviewed.

"We also talk about vicarious traumatization. Our concern is that kids will take on the trauma of the elder. [This type of training] helps students feel comfortable asking questions—they're not being invasive or violating their privacy. We talk about identification of symptoms—things they might be feeling the night after the interview.

"Finally, we play out scenarios of what to do if the interviewee starts crying. We tell them to give them time, give them space. Don't turn off the camera. Say, 'Take your time,' but don't feel the need to say anything or stop them from crying. Without this training, the young people may stop the interview or keep it going but stew inside and get nervous. Or they may react wrongly and say, 'Take a break,' which in many cases is the worst thing they can do. If the interviewee is crying, it means they are delivering authentic feelings and words. They can ask to stop, which of course we would. The best info often comes right after they cry."
—Project Director, *Telling Their Stories: Oral History Archives Project*

"A specialist came in to talk about vicarious traumatization. I stayed up nights thinking about it, and still do, but the benefits outweigh the disadvantages. With any traumatic experience, you grow, so it's just an exercise in growth. You can't go through life not being able to hear these stories, and that's just not realistic. I have a friend who won't watch documentaries about the Holocaust and it makes me angry. You can't shield yourself from history. You can't do anything about it if you don't know about it, no matter how sad and abysmal it is."
—Student participant, *Telling Their Stories: Oral History Archives Project*

- Interview skills and practice
- Personal goals
- General agreements
    - Be on time
    - What to do if you can't be here or complete a task
    - Dress and speak respectfully
    - Speak up—your input and questions are valuable!
- Consent forms
- Next steps
- Q & A

RESEARCH

Have you ever listened to a really great interview and wondered how the interviewer came up with their questions?

The answer is simple: Before the interview, they did their research. They found out what was going on historically during the subject's lifetime to get a basic understanding of what their life was like. If the subject has written a book, the interviewer has read it and found specific passages to comment upon. They've dug up what they can about the subject's family and personal life—anything and everything that will guide them in formulating questions that coax the subject to reveal relevant, detailed, juicy stories.

In short, as Zora Neale Thurston said, "Research is formalized curiosity. It is poking and prying with a purpose." Research helps interviewers excel at their craft. Not only can informed interviewers ask more pertinent questions, they will also have a better understanding of the interviewee's responses. If you omit this step, the interview may not flow as easily.

Here's a worst-case scenario, as reported by one project director. Because the young interviewer was not familiar with the topic, she didn't understand key terms and concepts that came up during the interview. She had to ask several questions just to understand the basic facts, wasting valuable interview time. The interviewee became increasingly impatient and irritable, finally scolding the young girl for her ignorance and lack of preparation. The connection between them was broken. The young interviewer no longer felt comfortable or confident and the interviewee felt that his experiences were not respected. All of this can and must be avoided by ensuring your interview team is fully prepared.

RESEARCH WHAT?

Ask yourself:
- What do I need to know in order to successfully shepherd this interview?
- What do I need to know in order to find out what I *don't* know?

Research Techniques

Think of research as a scavenger hunt. You have just enough information to know what to look for. Research techniques can include reading, field trips, seminars and presentations. One project director invited the author of a book on their reading list to come speak to their group of volunteers. As a result, the kids became more interested in the project; it also got them to read the book!

Ask the young people to put together and study a list of books and articles on the topic. Encourage them to look on the Internet—and beyond. Watch relevant documentaries or films that pertain to your subject matter. Consult maps of your area of interest and become acquainted with street names, rivers, or other geographical markers that may be pertinent to the interview. Better yet, take a field trip. Invite a local history expert to point out landmarks and explain the history.

Be specific. If you're talking to veterans, learn about the war they fought in. Get as much information as you can about the event or topic you hope to learn more about. Become familiar with some of the lingo so you recognize it and even utilize it in your questions.

FIELD TRIPS

"One goal of our project was for students to increase their knowledge of the people of Los Angeles and the history of migration to and within Los Angeles. We had a historian from USC who came to talk about why people moved to different places in the city.

"At the beginning of the project, we took students to the Autry National Museum, which has artifacts from different people who were here in the late 1880's.

"Our curriculum strategy was a scavenger hunt: find an artifact that reminds you of something from your life, something you wouldn't expect to see. We did a recording session there to tell the story of what it reminded them of from their life. They all made a very direct connection with other communities. For example, pots reminded them of grandparents' pots in Oaxaca."

—Project Director, *youTHink*

Interview Questions

The final stage of research is the preparation of the interview questions. You may have a general sense of what you want to find out at the onset of the project, but research will ensure that your questions are detailed and precise. Some projects ask the interviewers to come up with questions that interest them. Other projects provide the questions to the interviewers, and still others use a combination of both methods. It is always helpful to have at least two people work on the questions together. Your advisory team may want to contribute and the youth will also have an interesting point of view. Once your interviewer team has completed their research and is more knowledgeable about the subject matter, spend some time brainstorming the topics and specific details they want to learn more about.

In addition to considering content, take the time to craft your questions so they will bring the best responses. The formulation of interview questions is an art in itself; if you know an experienced interviewer or journalist, invite them help you. Basically, you want your questions to elicit more than a "yes or no" answer. The ideal question will open the door to the specific information you are seeking, and more.

Tips for framing interview questions

- Keep all questions open-ended:"How was that for you?" vs. "Did you like that?"
- Avoid leading questions: "How did you feel when that happened?" vs. "Wasn't that hard?"
- Be concise: This isn't about showing how much *you* know; it's about getting them to show you how much *they* know.
- Frame one question at a time: Avoid "When and where" questions. You'll only get one question answered anyway.
- Be specific: "Describe what was happening around you the night the war ended" vs. "Tell me about the war."

You may end up with a very long list of questions, and that's quite all right—as long as you don't expect to ask them all in every interview. Ideally you will start out with a long list and refine it for each interviewee as part of the pre-interview process defined in the next chapter.

List your questions by topic or chronology. This list is very helpful, even if you never once look at it during the interview. Even very experienced interviewers prepare a

HOW TO ASK THE RIGHT QUESTIONS

It may sound overly simple, but the best foundation for good interview questions is the old rule of thumb: **Ask Who, What, When, Where, Why and How.** Get details with phrases like:
- Tell me more about…
- Can you describe…
- Describe a typical…
- In what way…
- How did you feel about…
- What was happening around you when…
- What memory stands out the most from…

list ahead of time. As one professional interviewer noted, "I don't *need* to write them down—I know how to do this. But somehow the process of writing them down really does help."

A note about prepared questions: think of these questions as an outline or skeleton for the interview. They are there to help the interviewer stay on track and gather the necessary content. One of the most common mistakes an interviewer can make, however, is to stay glued to their list instead of reacting to what is happening in the moment. For this reason, remind your team that *these questions are just a starting point.* Once the subject starts talking, you get glimpses of new veins of information that need new questions to draw them out. This is often the most exciting part of the interview!

QUESTIONS FOR DIGGING DEEPER

- Can you tell me more about that?
- What happened after that?
- Describe what that looked/felt/sounded like.
- How did that make you feel?
- How do you feel about that now?
- What did you learn from that?

Once the interview questions are ready, make time for your interviewees to discuss their research methods and interview questions as a group. This discussion will both address any blind spots as well as broaden everyone's perspective and knowledge about the process and content.

The more creative and specific you are with your research strategies, the more the subject can come to life and therefore engage and inform your team. Whether they are young or old, they will be prepared and eager to take the next step.

LESSONS LEARNED: WORKING WITH YOUTH

Wish we had:

- More time! We just didn't have enough time with the students to really dig into the material.
- Remembered that student schedules change in the summer. We forgot to account for the crazy summertime schedules and basically had to delay the project until school started again in the fall.
- Reached out to more young people! We were worried that the teenagers wouldn't follow through, but they ended up being our most responsible volunteers.
- Spent more time on research. Our project would have been stronger had it been accompanied by some traditional research, as the students would have had more historical and factual context for their family stories.

So glad we…

- Put on a recruitment event at a local youth center. We only got one volunteer but the experience of speaking about the project really jazzed the kids who were already on board and made them more invested in the project.
- Took the time to clarify roles so the students were totally clear what they were supposed to do before, during and after each interview.
- Spent time practicing with our equipment. The kids were fascinated by the video camera and couldn't practice with it enough. During the interviews, they were able to change tapes and still keep the interview flowing.
- Talked openly about the emotional impact of interviewing and really prepared the kids to be both bold and sensitive in their interviews.

CHAPTER FIVE

Interviews

To be a person is to have a story to tell.

—Isak Dinesen

Interviewing truly is an art. Like the writer, the interviewer's task is to draw words from silence, seeking access into the castle of a stranger's mind. At the same time, interviewing is very simple—asking questions and listening to the response, something we all do many times a day. Every interview is alive, a unique improvisation. You walk the line between respectful and pointed. You listen with your eyes, ears, hands, and intuition. Sometimes you can practically smell the story, just under the surface of the words. You extract stories like an archaeologist extracts artifacts from the desert—gently, attentively, ambitiously. The best you can do is come prepared, relaxed, and ready to be surprised.

All of your preparation has been done to ensure that the right questions get asked in the right way at the right time, and that it's all recorded. Still, with a group of inexperienced interviewers and limited time, how can you ensure this will occur? The truth is, you cannot guarantee the success of your interviews; people are not predictable, recorders break, and even the best interviewers may not be able to get subjects to open up and reveal themselves and their experiences. Still, the better prepared your team is, the more likely your interviews will be deemed a success.

What constitutes a successful intergenerational interview? One that is a positive learning experience for the interviewer. One that allows the interviewee to feel comfortable enough to speak their truth. One that is successfully recorded! One that addresses the topics central to your project goals.

Some projects aim to get as many stories as possible. Others are seeking very specific information. Still others are providing a venue for people to talk about whatever is important to them. Many intergenerational oral history projects are more interested in building connections between the generations than collecting stories. Because of their differing goals, each of these projects will demand a different kind of interview style.

LISTENING VS. INTERVIEWING

"[For our project, the] volunteer is a listener, not an interviewer. This is their story, and what they tell us is what motivates them at this moment. We want to know what is important to them. We won't direct it. We've never had to provide prompts. Sometimes people have said, 'I don't have a story. I don't have anything to share with you.' If they'll agree to sit with me in their apartment for a moment, if there's a picture on the wall of Doris and her husband I'll say, 'Who's that?' and prompt a story like that.

"Some residents feel more comfortable with a structure. 'Where do I start?' they'll ask. I always answer, 'Wherever you want to.' I have a set of questions I can ask to put things into a chronology, but we don't push. I have a number of residents who say, 'That's too painful for me to talk about,' and you have to be sensitive to this."

—Project Director, *Life Storytelling Project*

CROSS INTERVIEWING

"We were doing the interviews [in the library] where we had a camera set up. We videotaped the person being interviewed, not the interviewer. I would ask a question and Gordon [an elder from the community] would answer, and we would go like that for a while. On a different day, Gordon asked me the questions and I would answer.

"We talked about a lot of different topics, from school to friends—all sorts of things, some of which we had talked about in his pre-interview. This cross interviewing definitely helped build a relationship. You can't have a connection with somebody unless both contribute. I think that me being interviewed was the more interesting to experience because…you start talking about your stories and experiences, and later if you have a chance to go back and look at it, you think, 'Ooh, I should have said this or I wish I had phrased it differently.' Still, it's a great chance to share your stories."

—Youth interviewer, *Fusing Identities*

CROSS INTERVIEWING

With cross interviewing, the interviewer and interviewee swap roles so both people interview each other. This technique can be useful for a variety of reasons. First of all, cross interviewing is an excellent way to learn and practice interview skills. There is nothing like being interviewed yourself to motivate you to refine your questions and interview style. Cross interviewing is also a good technique for helping people see the similarities and differences between their lives and situations. The connection between interviewer and subject deepens as they both learn about each other's lives.

GROUP INTERVIEWS

While it's tempting to collect all your interviews in one fell swoop, group interviews generally prove to be less effective than the more time-consuming but ultimately more productive one-on-one.

The more people talking, the less anyone will be heard. This is literally true with your equipment. Unless you have microphones for everyone, some people will be harder to hear than others. Even with individual mics for everyone, inevitably someone is sneezing or catching up with the person sitting next to them while another is speaking. Whispering voices and crinkling paper never seemed so loud as when you are in the middle of an interview!

Even more importantly, people may not feel as comfortable speaking up in a group. Many people are willing to say things to a relative stranger that they would never admit in front of their family members or friends. And, while it's true that interplay between subjects can be fascinating and can sometimes provoke memories and encourage reluctant people to open up, it can also lead to interruptions and contradictions that make people less willing to speak at all. In a group situation, the most dominant person usually ends up taking most of the interview time, even if they don't have as much to say.

Keep in mind as well that moderating a group interview requires a very experienced interviewer. Even then, group interviews are considered less valuable than a traditional interview and are not recommended within oral history methodology. Better to keep the group in one room while you do individual interviews somewhere else.

INTERVIEW SPACE

What's true with real estate is also true for interviews: location, location, location.

Your interview space should provide comfort and privacy so the narrator is able to relax and speak freely. Your audio recording is the most important recording so ensure the space is quiet, even if that means choosing a space that is smaller or less ideal for filming. Test your recording equipment in the interview location to make sure that it supports a live recording. Far too many interviews have been hampered by ambient noise. Ideally you can use and set up one space for all your interviews to create a controlled environment where these criteria are met. Often, however, you must travel to the subject's home or office. Wherever you are, your interview space should be:

- **Quiet:** No vrooming cars, people talking in the next room, or barking dogs. Turn off the phones and loud air conditioners. Do your homework and ensure that no loud meetings will be taking place next door at the time of your recording.
- **Private:** Create a safe environment by conducting the interview in a room where you cannot be overheard and there aren't many distractions, such as people walking by and looking inside. Remember that the interviewee may not want to be heard or seen during the interview.
- **The right size:** There's the interviewer and interviewee, cameraperson, project director, equipment, etc. Make sure your space is big enough for all these people and objects. You don't want to be cramped. At the same time, the acoustics in a huge room may not work either.
- **Indoors:** You have a much better chance to create and maintain a controlled environment inside and away from elements like wind, leaf blowers, traffic and other ambient noises.

Preparing the space

Once you've found the ideal space, it's time to think about how to set it up. Again, you are aiming for a private, safe and comfortable environment—but this is not the time to get too casual. Select chairs that are comfortable but not too squishy—better to sit around the dining room table than on the living room couch. Remove any squeaky furniture. Figure out where your camera, recorder and mics will go. You may have to move tables around so that both the interviewer and narrator can be easily heard, with emphasis on the narrator.

If you are filming the interview, find a backdrop that keeps the focus on the interviewee—nothing too loud or

LIGHTS, CAMERA, ACTION

- It can take years to master the many aspects of shooting film, but amateurs can shoot decent interviews by following a few basic guidelines.
- Remember that the focus of the shoot is the interviewee's *words*.
- Keep the camera still. Zooming in and out and changing the shot distracts away from what the subject is saying. This is about capturing the interview, not creative filmmaking.
- Wardrobe: unless you have a specific outfit or costume you want the subject to wear, advise them to dress simply, comfortably and respectfully. It seems obvious, but remind them that the video will be shared and made available for posterity so they'll want to wear something appropriate. In general, solid colors work better than busy prints. White doesn't film well but blue generally works well in any light. If you know the color of your backdrop, suggest colors that will stand out so your subject doesn't look like a head without a body.
- Choose a shot that includes the interviewee's face and hands, especially with a subject who uses lots of hand gestures.
- Keep the background elegant and sparse so that the focus remains on the interviewee. No windows, mirrors or reflective surfaces, busy paintings, or moving objects.
- Place the camera just behind the interviewer and shoot over the interviewer's shoulder to get a head-on shot of the subject.
- Remind the interviewee to look at the interviewer, not at the camera.

busy. Watch an interview show or a documentary and notice the kinds of backdrops and camera angles they use. If you don't like the walls in the background of your shot, move the interviewee in front of a bookcase or place plants or flowers on a table behind them. Play with the lighting in the room and check it on camera to find the most flattering levels. You may have to change the lighting levels for each person, depending on the time of day as well as their skin and hair color, make-up, and clothing. Make sure to give yourself plenty of time to create the look and feel you want for each interview.

INTERVIEW TEAMS

"For our project, we put the students together in interview teams of three to four kids who do their prep, research, interviews and follow-up together. Grouping kids makes it logistically easier to schedule interviews and made it possible for me to attend all of them since they weren't all happening at the same time. It also creates less pressure for each kid. They know that the product is going to be published on a website and accessible to the public, which puts a lot of pressure on them to do a great job. Having the kids work together adheres to our school's philosophy of collaborative learning. And it reflects the reality of learning styles: in a class situation, kids have different skills so the group interview style plays into that.

"Groups include one extrovert (who will probably be good at connecting with the elder and is also generally good at keeping the interview on track); one organizer (to keep the chronology of the interview); and one introvert who works the camera and equipment. All contribute equally to planning and research. All can ask questions in the interview while keeping their roles. The primary interviewer is responsible for the chronology of the interview. The secondary interviewer is responsible for listening for follow-up or questions of clarification—for example, questions that pertain to time and location. The cameraperson maintains the equipment and can also ask follow up and clarifying questions.

"The day before the interview, they meet to create their interview strategy and how they'll work together. In most cases, they'll decide to keep their roles throughout the entire interview, or they may choose to rotate roles for different topics."

—Project Director, *Telling Their Stories: Oral History Archives Project*

INTERVIEW TEAMS

Now that you have spent some time with your youth team, you can assess how best for them to work together. Depending on the complexity of the project and skills of your team, interviews can take place one-on-one or you can create interview teams. Less experienced interviewers often feel more at ease when they have a partner: someone who is taking notes, keeping time, and coming up with spontaneous questions. They may also need support with the equipment, especially if they are using a video camera.

Take some time to figure out how each individual can best succeed and then make sure everyone knows what they are supposed to do. You don't want two interviewers talking on top of each other and confusing the interviewee, or one interviewer who is so engrossed with the conversation they forget to turn over the tape in the video recorder.

In addition to the interviewer, the project director and/or manager may also want to be present during the interview to hear what is going on and ensure the necessary topics are covered. Your main concern is creating an atmosphere of safety where the subject speaks freely and you get it all on tape.

USING PHOTOGRAPHS OR PROPS

When utilized correctly, visuals can add a new dimension to your project. Take photos during the interviews to get some action shots. Posed photos with interviewer(s) and subject are an excellent addition to interview transcripts. It's also useful to have a visual of any objects that are spoken about. For example, one interviewee talked at length about the tiny shoes her mother wore after having her feet bound as a child. She brought a pair of the shoes with her and they were unbelievably tiny; seeing them really brought her story to life.

There are, however, a few common pitfalls to avoid when including objects in an interview. First of all, an audio recorder cannot see. Make sure you clearly identify the objects that are being discussed so there is no confusion. If possible, take a photo of the object or make a copy of the photo or document they've brought in so you can display it with the narrative. Secondly, clarify what will happen to the object during and after the interview. Can you touch it? Does the object relate to your interview questions or will it lead them on a tangent? Will they take it home with them right after the interview or can you hold onto it for an exhibition or to share with the rest of the team? If you want or need to keep the items brought in by an interviewee, create an object release form so everyone is very clear what will happen to it.[16] The items that people bring to such interviews are often very valuable to them, so make sure you are comfortable taking responsibility for them while they are in your care.

A third pitfall is figuring out which photos or objects to include. One interviewee showed up for his interview with a huge bag of photo albums and could hardly be deterred from going through every single one of them. The interview is not a place to choose visuals. Figure it out before the interview if possible (more on this below). If that's not possible, get your questions answered *before* letting them pull out the mystery objects.

Pre-interview

With so much to cover during the interview, in so little time, holding a pre-interview meeting can be the ideal way to clarify important details and begin to create a bond between interviewer and interviewee. Even the most experienced interviewers often meet with their subject before the interview. This may not be necessary if the interviewer and interviewee already know each other and are clear what they'll be talking about. For example, the Story Corps oral history project creates the space for two people who already know each other to record a 30-minute interview on the topic of their choice. They simply show up and start talking. For most projects, however, a pre-interview meeting can be extremely valuable, resulting in a more focused and open interview.

Ideally this meeting takes place a few days before the interview itself—close enough to keep the content fresh in

16. See Appendix 5 for Acquired Objects Form

your minds yet long enough to give you time to refine your questions. Depending on your project and interviewees, this can be a one-on-one meeting or other members of the project team may be present. Consider putting together a question list or worksheet to ensure all points get covered.[17] In some cases it may work to meet over the phone.

The purpose of the pre-interview meeting is to:

- Build rapport between the subject and interviewer
- Focus your content
- Clear up details

Build rapport

The best interviews occur when the interview subject opens up and speaks honestly and with depth about his or her views and experiences. The interview space can be very intimate. Very often, subjects are asked to talk about things they've never shared with another person, let alone a stranger, let alone a *young* stranger. Meeting someone for the first time can be awkward enough.

By meeting before the interview, this awkwardness is mitigated and both parties will feel more comfortable with

---

MAKING CONTACT

"The first telephone call when I actually phoned Gordon, I didn't know what to expect. I didn't know if I would get someone really nice, really grouchy—I just didn't know. He was really cool about it…. We talked about what he'd done as a teenager and where he'd lived, background stuff so I could get questions…. We didn't talk about specific details, just where did you live, in Colorado, which town, etc. Very basic background questions….

"That first contact with the person was really important because it helped build the possibility of a good interview."

—Youth interviewer, *Fusing Identities*

---

17. See Appendix 8 for sample Pre-Interview Worksheet

each other next time they meet. It also gives the interviewer some insight into the interviewee's voice volume, speaking style and any potential language barriers. This is also the time to ensure that each person understands their role and what they are expected to do. As a result, the interviewer is more willing to ask probing questions and the interviewee feels safe enough to open up.

Focus your content

Another reason to meet before the interview is to get a better idea of the information the interviewee possesses. One challenge of interviewing is knowing what to focus on—you have a limited period of time, it's very easy to go off topic, and all of the sudden you look up and it's time to go home. The pre-interview will help you avoid this common pitfall.

This meeting is your chance to find out which of your interview questions are pertinent. For example, several questions on the general list for the Oakland Chinatown Oral History Project had to do with attending school in Oakland Chinatown. In the pre-interview meeting, subjects were asked how old they were when they lived in Chinatown. If they moved there when they were older than eighteen years old, the school questions were irrelevant.

PRE-INTERVIEW MISHAP

The easiest mistake to make in a pre-interview meeting is to let the narrator tell their stories when you are not recording them. You want to find out what stories they have without actually hearing the story. Be direct! If your subject begins to get into it, cut in right away. You can say something like, "I'm really interested in that story, let's save it for the interview." Make a note of the story or frame a related interview question so you remember to bring it up during the actual interview.

In addition to helping the interviewer, this meeting will also prepare the interviewee for what they will be asked to talk about. Oftentimes people like to receive the questions ahead of time so they can excavate old memories without feeling on the spot. This is especially true when they are being interviewed by someone they don't know. It also gives you a chance to confirm what you *won't* be talking about so they will be less prone to irrelevant asides. Don't worry—no matter how honed and perfect your list of questions is, there will still be plenty of opportunity for spontaneity during the interview. The more focused your list, the more time you'll have for the "off list" questions that often bear the greatest fruit.

VALUE OF PRE-INTERVIEW MEETING

"First of all, the pre-interview was very important because it gave us a sense of what [the narrator's] background was so we could focus the questions on his adulthood, which was when he spent the majority of his time in Chinatown. We arranged a list, and we added some more questions that were related to his community-related activities as an adult. I think that preparation really helped us for this interview.... We also understood that he prefers to prepare ahead of time, so we were able to get that list of questions to him on time also."
—Youth interviewer, *Oakland Chinatown Oral History Project*

Clear up details

With the interview clock ticking away, you don't want to waste precious time procuring basic information. The pre-interview meeting is a better time to acquire basic biographical information and get the spelling for names and geographical landmarks.

In addition to interview content, you can cover the interview logistics. Clarify your interview time and location as well as how long the interview will take. Defer to the

Interview Timing

"We don't have a pre-interview meeting per se. What we do have to be careful about though is the timing. Do they sleep in the afternoon? Are they better after or before meals? We find out what time of day is best for them."
—Project Director, *Life Storytelling Program*

interviewee's schedule—it's vital that they be refreshed and energized for the duration of the interview, which can be surprisingly taxing.

If you are filming the interview, you may want to talk about wardrobe. When possible, show them the equipment you'll be using. Discuss what you want them to bring, especially if you're hoping for photos or memorabilia. This will save them time digging through boxes and increase the chances that they will actually bring the right items with them to the interview. Explain any forms and get them signed. Make sure they understand that they are agreeing to have

Explaining the Release Form

Some people feel uncomfortable asking participants to sign a release form. However you feel about it, take some time to get comfortable with the language you will use. As with all aspects of interviewing, the more comfortable you are, the better environment you create for the interview.

You can say something like this: "I want to let you know what we'll be doing with the recordings of your interview. We'll be keeping a copy here in our archives and they will also be available at the Des Moines Public Library in their oral history collection. That way, people and researchers who want first-hand stories about Des Moines can read or listen to your experience. At the end of our meeting today I'm going to ask you to sign a release form that allows us to utilize this recording in these ways."

their words recorded and that other people will be listening to them. If possible, let them know where the final products will be archived.

If the pre-interview meeting takes place in the same space where the interview will be recorded, take some time to check out the space. Look out for how you'll rearrange the furniture, if necessary, and what you'll need to bring, such as extra lighting, props for the backdrop, or padding to muffle noises.

Most importantly, take the time to answer their questions. Remind them what will happen to their words after the interview in a way that makes them feel comfortable and hopefully gratified by their contribution.

THE INTERVIEW

After all your preparations, the day is finally here! Before the interviewee arrives, check all of your equipment to make sure everything is in working order and that you have extra batteries and power cords. If you have access to the interview space before the interviewee arrives, make sure it is all set up before they get there: comfortable room temperature, chairs, tables and recording devices in place, backdrop, cameras and lights ready.

If you are interviewing at the subject's home or workplace, which is becoming more and more common, ensure that you have ample time for set-up—at least thirty minutes, more if you've never seen the location or need to set up lights or backdrop. Remember that the most important aspect of recording is sound, so choose the quietest space, even if it is a bit cramped or less ideal visually.

Let people in surrounding rooms know that you are recording and ask them to keep as quiet as possible for the duration of the interview. Turn off the air conditioner and the ringers on all phones—but before you do, let office or housemates know what you're up to so they don't turn them back on or wonder why it got so hot all of the sudden.

Hang up your "interview in progress sign" and you're ready to go.

Interview checklist

- ☐ Water and glasses
- ☐ Pen and paper
- ☐ Tissues
- ☐ Recording equipment, including a back-up recorder
- ☐ Camera
- ☐ Tripod
- ☐ Extra batteries
- ☐ Power cord and /or extension cord
- ☐ Backdrop
- ☐ Consent form
- ☐ Acquired Objects form
- ☐ List of interview questions
- ☐ Photos and other interview props, if using
- ☐ Sign for door: Interview in progress, please don't disturb

The interview clock starts ticking the moment the interviewee arrives. The longer you take to get settled, the less time you have for the interview. Try to keep things moving without noticeably rushing. Find out if they need anything before you begin and get them a glass of water. Put pens and paper in front of them so they can draw or write as needed during the interview. Let them know that you've turned off the AC and phones and double check that their cell phones are turned off too. Do your mic and light level checks, and get started.

A quick note about nerves. It's very normal to be nervous before an interview. You've done all this prep and people are

---

PRACTICE TIP

Role-play the interview prep in addition to the interview. See how it feels to be the narrator ushered into the interview space and ask yourself what you would like in that situation. Also, spend some time practicing with your equipment so you can set up and perform the mic and light level checks quickly and easily wherever you go.

counting on you to get the information they need. You don't have much time and you cannot predict what the interviewee will come at you with. Don't worry! Even the pros get nervous. It's a good sign. Some would say it's necessary and even helpful, providing you with an extra boost of energy. Still, if you are feeling queasy, do your best to appear calm when the narrator arrives. Young or old, it's the interviewer's role to lead the way. Most of all, enjoy the experience!

Interview tips

- **Begin every interview the same way.** State the date and location of the interview, the full names of the interviewer and interviewee, and the name of the project. If necessary, have the subject spell their name out. "This is Joseph Canon interviewing Anna Lee on June 24th, 2009, at the Main Street Community Center. This is the first interview being recorded for the Main Street Oral History Project."
- **Start with easy questions.** Start off with simple biographical queries and give yourself time to get the interview flowing before digging into tougher or more emotional questions.
- **Be flexible.** Use your list of questions as a general guide but don't be constrained by them or your ideas of how the interview should go.
- **Let them do the talking**. As much as possible, keep your introductions, explanations and questions brief to allow more time for the narrator to speak. To show that you are listening, nod your head instead of responding with Oohs and Ahhs. Any sound you make will be picked up by the recorder and could muffle the narrator's words.
- **Put blank paper and pen in front of interviewee**, not so much to capture what they actually draw or write, but to help them remember things. For example, drawing a map of their neighborhood might help them recall other details about it.
- **Refrain from interrupting** or making comments or judgments about what you've heard. Remember, this interview is about them and their views, not yours.

- **Go off-list.** Your list of questions is only a guide. Stay focused on what the interviewee is saying and ask questions that relate to what is being expressed in the moment.
- **Allow for some tangents.** Sometimes it can seem that the interview is going off track, but circumlocutions can often lead to the best stories. If it keeps going farther off the track, nudge the conversation back to the topic at hand.

PREPARED VS. SPONTANEOUS QUESTIONS

"I think it's important to have the questions not only prepared but to be spontaneous with the questions. I would say that using your list of questions is like using a flashlight to look in a dark room. It's great when you point the beam ahead. But if you don't move it around, you won't see everything that's there. Who knows, there could be a pile of gold or chocolate hidden in the corner!

"To move away from the scripted questions can be hard, I know. One thing I would recommend is to interview someone you know as practice—someone you know pretty well but not super well, like a friend at school. That way you know some stories already and can ask spontaneously, rather than just sticking to your questions."

—Youth Interviewer, *Fusing Identities*

- **Give plenty of time for responses.** Your silence is an invitation for them to say more. Don't be afraid of gaps in the conversation!
- **Be aware of your body language**. As the interviewer, you are the audience. The narrator will appreciate and respond well to an audience that is actively engaged. You don't want to slump in your seat, yawn, or look everywhere but at the narrator. At the same time, they probably don't want to be stared at. Everyone is different so find a balance that works for your narrator.

- **Ask one question at a time**.
- **Follow up.** If the interviewee gives a short answer or makes a general statement, follow up and ask for more details. Ask, "Why?" or "Why not?" Request more information by saying, "Could you explain that in more detail?" "Can you give me an example of that," or "Please say more."
- **Ask for definitions.** Look out for words that have critical meaning for the interview. For example, if the narrator mentions using a beet shovel, ask for more information. What does a beet shovel look like? How was it used? What was its purpose? Did everyone have one or was it a specialty item? With the right questions, a simple description of an object or definition of a word can lead to great, detailed stories.
- **Be persistent.** If you must, rephrase and re-ask important questions several times to get the full amount of information
- **Keep track of your recording device(s).** Some people liken the recording devices to a third participant in

---

ONE OBJECT, MANY STORIES

"We were talking about jobs Gordon had held. He mentioned to me that he had different jobs during school. In the interview, he mentioned that he had worked in beet fields. I asked him more about that and he had a great story about how you go out to the fields with this tool with a wicked curve at the end of it, and you have to throw it down on the ground. What ended his work in the beet fields was him throwing this tool down and tearing his knee open. That ended his career.

"Part of it was just that this was not something I'd ever thought about. I live in the suburbs and don't harvest beets ever. It was so removed from my experience; it was a brand new thing and this was intriguing to me."
—Youth Interviewer, *Fusing Identities*

the conversation. Without giving them too much attention, you need to keep them in mind. For example, if the narrator speaks quietly, you may need to move the recorder closer to them or ask them to speak up. You also need to check the recorders from time to time to make sure they're still recording; you may need to pause to turn over or change tapes. The trick is to do so without distracting the interviewee and unnecessarily reminding them that they are being recorded. Avoid playing with or looking at the recorders while they are talking. You don't want to convey that the recorder is more important than they are.

- **Remember context.** Others who will be listening to this interview may not have as much knowledge as you do. Ensure that all references are clarified. If they say, "Joe did that," follow up by clarifying, "Joe your brother?" In addition, remember to be the "eyes" for those who will read the transcripts later. For example, if someone says, "Oh, it was about this long," and gestures with their hands, follow up by saying, "So that would be about three feet long?"

- **Jot down your questions as they arise** so you can follow up at the appropriate time without interrupting.

- **Maintain eye contact.**

- **Don't worry if your questions don't come out as eloquently as you'd like.** Your lack of perfection may actually make them more comfortable!

- **Keep the recorder on for the entire interview.** Sometimes people remember details or new stories after the interview has concluded. If you've already turned off your recording devices, invite the narrator to pause until you get them recording again.

- **Take breaks as needed.** Watch to see if the interviewee is becoming tired or uncomfortable. Especially with older people, a break after 45 minutes will be very appreciated.

- **Keep interviews to a maximum of 90 minutes.** It is surprisingly taxing to talk and listen intently for extended periods.

- **Hold your ground.** Don't be intimidated by subjects who you assume to be more learned or famous than you. Know your stuff and keep an attitude of respectful equality.
- **Don't intimidate the interviewee.** Sometimes an official oral history project can seem frightening, especially to people who don't feel they have contributed much to history. Make a connection to their life to show that you value who they are.
- **Don't be afraid to ask personal, probing questions.** Ask them with respect and give them ample time to respond. If they don't answer, return to the same topic later.
- **Save the tough or more personal questions for the end** of the interview, after the interviewee has become more comfortable with you.
- **End the interview with finality**. Ask if there is anything else they'd like to talk about and if there are any other questions that you should ask them. When you are well and truly done, say, "Thank you, this interview is now over."
- **Minimize the number of interviews per day**. The room is all set up and your interviewers are on site, making it very tempting to schedule a bunch of interviews one after the other. Avoid the temptation. Interviews are hard work, mentally, emotionally and even physically if you are handling equipment or sitting on hard chairs. Keep it to a maximum of two interviews per day.

MEANINGFUL INTERVIEW MOMENTS

"A meaningful moment to me is that pin-dropping silence that happens when we do the interviews. Most of the interviews were done with small groups.... When someone was telling an emotional story, everyone was really glued to it. If a student started to cry—we don't have a lot of this so it might have been their first exposed crying—I noticed how present and attentive and kind everyone was. Not surprising, but lovely."

—Project Director, *youTHink*

DIGGING DEEPER

"One of the most striking moments was when I was interviewing Warren, one of the company commanders of the Rainbow Division that liberated the Dachau camp. He was telling us about the moment when they entered the camps. He was twenty years old when he did this, and I was eighteen when I interviewed him, and this really made me see the extreme difference in our lives: his sorrowful experience that I would never have, and taking the time out of his day to tell me about it. There was a disconnect in our experiences, during the connection of the interview. He was my age when these things were happening to him.

"Like I said, Warren was the company commander —clearly a strong man and an important figure. He'd told his story hundreds of times, to young and old people, for books, for other oral history projects. At one point, he was talking about how he still has nightmares twenty years after the experience. He started shaking and almost cried. I was so surprised that a man with such a full life would still be so moved and affected by his experiences. This proved to me that history is not an isolated series of events that are stuck in the past: it's not just in textbooks and archives but in people's hearts and minds. I felt like I had a duty to share that with other people so they could have a comparable experience. My responsibility as an oral historian at that moment was to listen patiently, record it and make it available to other people.

"When he got to liberating Dachau, he breezed through it and we had to go back. 'When you first entered, what exactly did you see and smell?' I tried to phrase the questions as innocuously as possible and use as gentle a tone as possible so he'd be detailed in his descriptions. More a matter of tone: I didn't want to be abrupt. I would let him finish his thought first, then say, 'Before, you were mentioning about being at the gate in Dachau. Would you tell me more about how you felt at that moment?' Or, 'If you could put yourself back in your 20-year-old shoes what would you say then versus what you would say today?'"

—Youth Interviewer, *Telling Their Stories: Oral History Archives Project*

- **Above all, be a good listener**. Allow the interviewee time to think and be respectful of their words, whether you agree with them or not.

Tips for Interviewing Elders

While these pointers are often true for an interview subject of any age, they are especially relevant to elders.

- **Look for signs of fatigue.** Participating in an interview takes a surprising amount of energy. You might think that because you're just sitting down and talking, you could go on all day. On the contrary: whether you are the narrator or the interviewer, interviews take an enormous amount of energy and focus. The more tired they are, the less your interviewees will be able and willing to remember and articulate details. It's better to shorten the interview or take more breaks than to cram too much into too little time.

- **Schedule the interview at their ideal time of day.** For some, mornings are best. Others do better in the afternoon. Find out when your subject feels most alert and energized and schedule all meetings within that time frame.

- **Be sensitive to difficulties hearing, speaking and remembering.** All too often, the inability to hear, speak clearly, or remember is interpreted as lack of intelligence. This couldn't be further from the truth. It is the interviewer's job to speak clearly and audibly, without shouting. Maintaining eye contact helps. Be prepared to repeat yourself. Let the elder set the pace, and be respectful and patient as you listen.

- **Refrain from using too much modern slang.** Even if they speak the same language, youth and elders may speak a very different dialect. Phrases and slang that are common today may not make sense or may sound disrespectful to someone of another generation.

- **Ensure the room temperature is comfortable for all.** How is it possible that a room can be cold to one person and sweltering to another? It's not only possible; it happens all the time. Find a setting that works for everyone, with priority going to the elder.

- **Don't get lost in technology.** Young people are often more familiar and comfortable with gadgets. The same recorders, computers and cameras that young people love can be intimidating to elders. While the interviewer does need to ensure their equipment is functioning properly, the focus should remain on the interviewee, not the machines.

- **Respect your elders.** This point essentially covers all the previous points. While this important tenet is becoming less common in today's society, it is invaluable for the interviewer to practice both inside and outside the interview space.

Common interview conundrums

How do you address your narrator? Use honorific terms or call them by their first name or nickname? The general answer to this is to be respectful but not too distant. Take your cues from the interviewee. Some prefer formality, while others do not. If they invite you to call them by their first name, go right ahead.

How do you deal with the "stale story" that the subject has told a thousand times before? Let them tell it the way they always do—then follow up with questions. "That sounds really funny. Were there any challenges you faced at that time as well?"

How long do I wait for the narrator to answer? Silence is very important in an interview. Keeping silent shows your confidence as well as giving your subject time to think. Unlike social conversations, interviews are strong enough to bear silence. Give it a little room to see what happens. If it becomes uncomfortable or squirmy, jump in.

What if they don't have much to say? Some interviews are going to be better than others—this is true for experienced and novice interviewers alike, and accepting this fact will take the pressure off. Still, you can help by being prepared with a long list of questions. If you don't immediately get a detailed answer, try asking the question in many different ways. Be sure to strike the balance between probing and allowing for silence and short answers. Gentle coaxing can help as long as you stay respectful. If they still don't have much to say, keep the interview short and move on.

What if they keep talking after the interview is over? Turn that recorder back on! Or, as in the pre-interview meeting, let them know that you really want to hear that story so can they save it for the next interview? Make a note to bring that story up next time.

How do you get sometime to tell you about the silver lining to their hard times? Sometimes people can get mired in their memories of misery. Ask questions that dig deeper than the circumstances themselves, such as, "What did you say to yourself at that time to get through it?" and "What did you learn from that?" Go for what they gained through their experience.

What if they start to cry? Many young people are eager to hear great stories but are afraid of "making" the narrator cry. For this reason, they may not be willing to ask the hard, probing questions. While most interviewers are not trying to get their subjects to cry, it is often a good sign that the subject is opening up and sharing stories that are very meaningful to them. It is a sign of trust. Don't turn off the recorder. Don't rush in with words or condolences. In fact, don't do anything. Let them cry in silence. Give them the space to be with their emotions and tell you what provoked them. And please don't feel guilty. You are probably helping them more than you know.

POST-INTERVIEW

After all your hours of prep, in a blink of an eye the interview is over. Chances are you are both elated and exhausted. Before heading home, however, take a few minutes to wrap everything up. Before your narrator leaves, make sure you've taken the photos that you want. Make a list of all the

THE POWER OF SHARING STORIES

"I remember one boy telling a story about his grandfather who got pretty emotional. It wasn't a shameful thing; it's that he never realized what his family went through. Same with another girl—while she was reciting it, I guess she was also listening to what she was saying and it surprised her and it finally hit her that what her parents went through was a reality—not just a story that she read—and it made her cry.

"For me, the story I chose I had heard since I was small; I just wanted to save it as precisely as I could. It was about my mother's side of the family coming to America during the time of the riots and war going on in El Salvador, when there was a problem, when America was invading and they feared the Communist idea that El Salvador was spreading.

"The civil war had a lot of families barricading themselves in their houses. Bullets were going everywhere. They would barricade their door with mattresses and never go outside. Piles of bodies were left in the middle of the street as a warning to others. A lot of kids were being forced into the war. Mothers said, 'We cannot allow this to happen to our children,' so they made it here safe and sound.

"To get themselves here I know was very hard. They don't talk about it a lot because I guess it brings back a lot of bad memories. They were stuck in the house for over a month and were very sick and lonely and weak and pale. I remember my cousin telling me that it was hell, literally hell, and she never wants to go through that again. I am just thankful."

—Student participant, *youTHink*

items they've brought with them to the interview. If you are borrowing any items, give them an Acquired Objects form to sign and clarify verbally when and how the objects will be returned. Remind them of the next steps and invite them to any follow-up events. Make sure you have their address to send them a thank you note.

After saying good bye to the interviewee, jot down any notes you want to remember or that will help with your next steps while the stories are still very fresh in your mind. Six months from now or even tomorrow morning you may not remember everything quite so clearly. Label all your cassettes, CD's or digital files with the names of the interviewer and interviewee, date, location and project title.

There is something very magical in the air after an interview. This sharing of stories can be exhilarating for the mind and the soul. Even though you're tired, this is a great time to talk about what you've experienced in the interview. This is especially true for intergenerational projects, where the young interviewer's experience is as important as the oral histories they collect. Have a debrief conversation about the interview process and content.

You can even interview the interviewers. Find out what they learned, what surprised them, and how they feel about the whole experience.[18] For the Oakland Chinatown Oral History Project, these post-interviews were a last-minute idea that ended up providing some of the best and most inspiring content, reinforcing everyone's resolve and motivating the whole team to keep moving forward.

SOLIDIFY THE LEARNING

"The best teaching often comes after the interview, when you debrief."
—Project Director, *Telling Their Stories: Oral History Archives Project*

When young people conduct an intergenerational oral history interview, they may well find themselves more interested in talking to the other elders in their lives. Hopefully this experience will provoke them to talk to their own family or continue to meet with the person they interviewed. As one young interviewer said, "I don't get a chance to hear the stories of my family and the people who came before me and made

---

18. See Post-Interview Question list in Appendix 9.

UNEXPECTED REWARDS

Project Manager: What did this experience teach you?
Youth Participant: Well, I know for a fact that if you don't find out more, the history won't be learned at all. Just by looking at an elder, you might not think there's a lot to be told. But then, if you really go into their life, you will find out a lot of different stories to be told.

That's the same thing with my grandma. On the outside, she just talks and talks about nothing. But then I found out later—I might even interview her later—but I found out that she's part of some Communist thing and she actually rebelled against Mao Zedong [and] got beaten up and got thrown into jail. I would never know that just by looking at her or by hearing her talk. If you delve into her life, you'll find out so much about her life.

Project Manager: How does knowing her history change your feelings towards her?
Youth Participant: It definitely changed me or definitely changed my feelings toward her because—like I said, I look at her, I see her as a grandma. But then, the fact that she rebelled and she was kind of like, maybe a hippie. She definitely rebelled a lot. I see my grandma way different—probably cool. (laughter)

—Project Manager and Youth interviewer, *Oakland Chinatown
Oral History Project*

me who I am today. My grandmother lives in another country and I don't even speak her language. I may never get to talk to her, but now I want to ask my mom about her so at least I know something." Even if they don't pursue relationships with elders, and even if elders don't pursue relationships with teenagers, they may find a growing respect for one another. This is, after all, the true goal.

LASTING CONNECTION

"I hadn't met Gordon before the project. After interviewing him, he offered to drive me home and it turns out he lives about four or five blocks away from me. It was really intriguing to see that this really cool guy has lived so close to me for years and years and I've never seen him before! There are interesting people all over, but if you don't make the effort to connect with them, you'll never find them. I wished that I could have connected more with him after the interviews, but he died three months after. I felt pretty bad, actually. It was like losing a friend. Still, I'm really glad I met him and got to talk to him....

"There's another guy who worked on the project...and he still corresponds with the guy who interviewed him, or they did for at least a year after the project. It wasn't just this one-time random encounter; it was an actual building of a relationship that maintained itself even after the events that brought the people together were over. It's important not to lose contact with that person. Keep talking with them. Don't just give up the ghost and let it go. More than likely, you've found a friend. I got to talk to Gordon one more time, and I wish that I had had the time to do more.

"The project really made me wish I could have talked to my dad's father, who died before I was born. My grandfather was about the same age as Gordon and he grew up in similar small town rural communities. My grandpa was a World War II veteran, and I just wish I could have talked to him. Right after the project, me and one of my friends who'd also done the project were talking with a mutual friend whose relative was in the hospital. Because we had both gotten so much from the project, we both urged her to go talk to her relative while she still could.

"If you don't connect with other people, you don't fully experience life. If you don't connect with people, you're missing out on 90% of what the world is. That's really what life is: your relationship with other people—whether it's over the Internet or in a schoolroom or across a minefield—your relationship with other people is what shapes the world."
—Youth Participant, *Fusing Identities*

LESSONS LEARNED: INTERVIEWS

Wish we had...

- Spent more time focusing on and practicing spontaneous questions. Several of the students were nervous during the interviews so they stayed glued to their list of questions.
- Remembered to check the recorder during the interview. It was only after the subject had come and gone that we discovered the recording had stopped about midway through!
- Stopped the interviewee from telling her stories at the pre-interview meeting. When we got to the actual interview, the stories sounded very stale and many details were omitted.
- Invited less people to listen in on the interviews. They made so much noise it was very distracting and actually interfered with the recording.

So glad we...

- Checked not only the interview room but also the rooms on either side. It turned out that there was supposed to be a big meeting in the next room at the time of our interview, which they were able to change to another location so we'd have the quiet we needed.
- Started doing pre-interview meetings to give the students a chance to meet and get comfortable with the person they'd be interviewing.
- Paired the kids up so they could work on their interview questions together. It saved us a lot of time and helped the kids bond as well as practice new skills.
- Asked the interviewee to write down the place names he was referring to. Some of them were tiny villages that we couldn't even find on a map afterwards.
- Recorded the post-interviews with the students. This material provided so much inspiration for the rest of the team.

CHAPTER SIX

Archiving

"The story was the bushman's most sacred possession. These people knew what we do not; that without a story you have not got a nation, or culture, or civilization. Without a story of your own, you haven't got a life of your own."

—Laurens Van der Post

A software engineer once told me that in his world, if data is stored in only one place, it doesn't *exist*. In order for it to exist, it must be stored in at least two different places. Although I won't go so far as to challenge the existence of oral histories based on their storage, I would agree that at least two copies is a very good idea. Databases disappear, buildings burn, humans err. Archiving will help ensure that your hard work does still exist in the foreseeable future.

"Archive" is both a verb and a noun. An archive is a repository of documents, hard copy or digital, as well as the act of placing materials in such a repository. For oral histories, this step of preservation is just as important as conducting the interview itself; an interview that cannot be shared is just like that proverbial tree falling silently in the woods. According to my engineer friend, if you don't archive it, it simply ceases to exist.

In addition to preserving oral histories, the archive serves another critical function: providing access. Placing your oral histories in an archive will make them accessible to the public. This access to primary source materials has shifted perspective on the value of oral history; historians and academics who once frowned on oral history as a research methodology are now more frequently accepting oral histories as qualitative research. Preserving and creating access to these materials is by far the most important reason for conducting oral histories in the first place. As a librarian said, Why go to all that trouble if no one will ever see it again? She has a point.

PRIMARY SOURCE MATERIALS

Primary source materials provide first-hand accounts of events, practices, and experiences. Generally speaking, such materials are created by actual witnesses or participants in the events being described. Primary source materials include letters, photos, and diaries as well as accounts that were documented after the event, such as memoirs and oral histories. They are considered the most valuable research tool for historians and others because:

- Primary sources give *firsthand* information about the past.
- The narrator actually witnessed and experienced the event in question.
- Primary source documents accurately represent that person's point of view.
- Primary source materials allow historians and others to formulate their own hypotheses or analyses without being clouded by the interpretations or opinions of others.
- Primary sources are the foundation from which all secondary texts are produced. The function of secondary sources, such as textbooks, articles and documentaries, is to interpret primary sources.

In truth, oral histories are sometimes the only means for documenting and making available the histories of "invisible" communities. For example, the LGBT community is notoriously under documented. Researchers looking for historical data about the lesbian community in the 1940's, '50's and '60's, for example, won't find anything in the library because it was never talked or written about. Now, oral historians are going back to collect and preserve those stories.

ARCHIVING—LONG TERM BENEFITS

"The value of archiving is that we are preserving things for the very long-term future. Oral historians are usually excited about an immediate goal like an exhibition, or bringing the community together. But they are also producing an historical document, whether that's intentional or not, which will be very useful for people and researchers far into the future. Aren't we glad documents have been preserved from the Middle Ages? They really help us understand the past. Our oral histories will help future people understand who we are. We are really in it for the long run.

"As far as short-term benefits, we process information for the archive so it can be used right now as well as in the future. Anything preserved and made available, which is the goal of libraries, is useful always."

—Nancy MacKay, author of *Curating Oral Histories: From Interview to Archive*

As this book has shown, there are all kinds of oral history projects. Many of them consider preservation, but fewer put energy into providing accessibility. Projects are often geared towards the participants only. They may not even know how valuable their work is, or it may seem relevant only to a contained population. The truth is, people's stories can be relevant far beyond the realms of those they touch directly. Even small details can have enormous impact. Historians, researchers, students, journalists, writers, storytellers, archaeologists, anthropologists, historical societies, museums, and libraries—including the Library of Congress—are just some of the many people and institutions that can benefit from your hard work.

The first step in archiving your work is deciding how you'd like to preserve it. Nancy MacKay, archivist and author of *Curating Oral Histories: From Interview to Archive*, recommends that you initiate contact with potential archives

NO ARCHIVE, NO HISTORY

"We've had some graduate students come to the center to access transcripts for their research. They wanted to find out about how Chinatown was affected by the urban renewal policies of the city government. One student wanted to know what happened here in 1960's and 1980's and there was very little historical data available. She combed through our transcripts to distill historical data in addition to information about how urban renewal affected the community members.

"Even when it is not a formal academic approach to documentation, oral history is important and helpful. When there is little or no documented history, such as in this case, oral history is all you have. And, our overall history of a community or a people is truly a collected collection of our general history. The history of African-Americans is missing because so many individual stories are missing.

"There are so many stories missing from the Asian-American community. Some people believe that Chinatown as a community has been ignored by government entities because they have not spoken up and documented their history. Like this student was researching, a large part of the local community was displaced in the '70's to make way for a new public transit system. People were forced to leave their homes to make way for a subway station. They just accepted their fate; even though it was traumatic, they did it. Now, no one even knows this happened. This is not an atrocity on the scale of other things that have happened, but it does show what goes on with the human memory. All it takes is one generation. If the history is not preserved, it's as if it never happened."

—Project Director, *Oakland Chinatown Oral History Project*

at the very beginning of your project. Libraries are a great place to start as many of them house oral history collections. It's not always simple to get yours added to the collection, however, which is why she suggests you find out exactly what they require. Ideally, you can partner with the library. The oral historian's role is to provide accurate data and files that are correct, well labeled, and in the right format. The librarian's job is to preserve what they are given. They can only do as good a job as the information that is presented to them.

Once a partnership is set up between a library and oral history project team, they work together to develop a template for information gathering.[19] With the information provided by the oral historian, the library's archiving team creates access points to the material by cataloging and indexing the information. A catalog describes if the library has a certain oral history, if that oral history is available, and how you can find it (for example, online or a particular physical location). An index, on the other hand, is a form of detailed subject access, pointing to specifically designated topics within the oral history itself. An index can be created from the recorded interview or from the transcript and should include time references to where that topic can be found in the recording (for example, beet farming: CD 3, 12:14:08). The more information you provide, such as the topic of the oral history, names of the interviewers and interviewees, name of project, and other subtopics covered in the interview, the more access points can be created.

Libraries are but one potential repository for your project. Many universities house oral history collections and actively support oral history programs. Oral history programs are a cross between a library and an oral history project and are often devoted to accepting projects from the community. They can be an excellent liaison for archiving as well as offer support with legal forms and other aspects of oral history work.[20] For example, Baylor University's Institute for Oral History houses

---

19. See Appendix 10 for a sample Cataloging Template
20. See Appendix 11 for an Oral History Program List

many oral histories within its archives, makes their catalogs accessible via their website, and offers workshops, documents and oral history grants and fellowships.

ACCESSIBILITY

Traditionally, many libraries have kept their oral histories in special collections; people who wanted to access them had to come to the library itself as the materials were not allowed off the library grounds. More and more, though, the trend these days is to make data available online, a real boon for oral histories and the people who utilize them. Many online oral histories are a hybrid of indexing and cataloging; they include both a descriptive record of the interview as well as direct access to the transcript and/or recording itself.

Most libraries also include catalogs of their holdings in a worldwide library catalog called WorldCat®, a database of the works housed in thousands of libraries around the world.[21] While not every library catalogs their collections in this database, many do so it's a good place to look for research materials available through libraries worldwide. You can access oral histories on this site by doing a search for the name of the project, the sponsoring institution, or even the name of a specific interviewee. By contacting the specific library you can gain access to the actual works. This is just one tool that libraries utilize to create access to their holdings.

Making it happen

Because of the varying archival practices and procedures, it's best to identify the repository you hope will house your collection at the onset of your project. As soon as you've determined your ideal location, contact them to make an appointment to talk about your project and find out if they are interested in archiving it for you. Some libraries are actively collecting oral histories while others are not. Some libraries take whatever they can get, while others have strict

---

21. See the WorldCat website at www.WorldCat.org

restrictions. Every archive has a different set of stipulations and requirements for accepting your work. They may have a preference for certain topics, such as local history or stories from a particular sector of the community. Find out what they need.

Find out also what they will require from you in addition to the oral histories themselves. As mentioned before, some libraries provide a data sheet for you to fill out that includes contact information and details about the project to be used for cataloging. Make sure that you spell all proper names correctly because catalogers must rely on the information you supply. At the very least, they will also need signed release forms. They may also want to speak with you about rights management. Although this is negotiable, libraries often want the copyright on oral history materials. By holding the copyright, the library can give permission for others to reprint or reuse the material, instead of forcing them to track down the specific project director and interviewees who often cannot be found.

In addition to partnering with a library, oral history program, or other repository, you should also create your own archive. All materials should be stored together in a safe, locked, dark, cool space that is moisture free. Label everything clearly. And of course, make two copies of everything.

TRANSCRIPTS

The recording is the primary document in an oral history project, but it's not very user-friendly. The most accessible form of an interview is the transcript, which is a verbatim rendition of the audio or video interview—basically, a direct translation from spoken to written word. The transcript is considered a secondary document because no transcript can be exactly the same as a recording. For example, most transcripts lack speech patterns and intonations, so while the content is the same, the reader of the transcript cannot get a sense of how the words sounded. That being said, a transcript is infinitely easier to use than a recording. Instead of rewinding and fast-forwarding blindly through a recording, the user can flip through the pages to easily find the segment they want.

In addition to ease of use, archivists see another function for transcripts. The paper format is considered a preservation format. In our digital age, it's also common to consider digital formats for preservation and this is certainly a great idea. However, formats change over the years and technology that was very common fifty years ago is already obsolete. It's great to have an audio collection of your community's oral histories, but if it's all on 8-track tape you're going to have a hard and potentially expensive time listening to it today.

Still, digital materials are becoming more and more accessible through the Internet. In addition to digital archives such as WorldCat, many oral history projects build their own websites to share their content online, making it very easy for the public to access primary sources, such as recordings, videos and photographs, as well as written transcripts. To cover your bases, it is recommended to archive your materials both in a paper and digital format.

Regardless of what you plan to do with your recordings, it's wise and very helpful to create transcripts. It's also time-consuming. It generally takes about three to six hours to transcribe every hour of recorded interview. If you plan or hope to create transcripts, be sure to budget enough time or money for this service.

Transcribing is not terribly difficult but does require accuracy, good typing skills, and careful attention to detail. There are professional transcriptionists who can whip through interviews but their services can be costly. If you include transcribing in the responsibilities of your volunteers, make sure they have the support and time they need. Some projects include transcription in the responsibilities of the interviewers. In this case, it's ideal for the interviewer to type up the transcript soon after the interview is recorded, while the details are still fresh in their minds. This solidifies their learning, both about interviewing skills as well as the topics discussed. The interviewer also has a better chance of understanding odd turns of phrase and mumbles since they have the context of the entire experience to guide them.

Another option is to bring in other volunteers to do the transcriptions. The work of transcribing is very intimate and much can be gained from hearing the stories firsthand. Whoever types up the transcript, once they've finished transcribing the interview they should always listen to the recording one more time while comparing it to the transcription to ensure they haven't left anything out or made any obvious errors.

Transcripts are usually formatted in a dialogue form, like a play.[22] The interviewer's questions and comments are included with the narrator's responses. Each page is labeled clearly with the name of the project.

Remember that the goal is to get these transcripts into as many hands as possible, so you want to make them user-friendly. Your local library may have other ideas or requirements as well.

TEENAGE TRANSCRIBERS

"We were given free online software that helps you do the transcripts. Regular teen volunteers did all the transcripts. They weren't involved in the interviews so they also got to hear the interviews. They found it quite interesting; they liked to hear stories of people talking about their lives. They came in and were very happy to do the transcribing. All they needed was the ability to type. Once we made the formatting clear, they all had a good sense of what needed to be done."

—Project Director, *Fusing Identities*

Editing transcripts

Typing up a transcript sounds very straightforward—you simply type whatever the subject says, right? In truth, it's

22. See Appendix 12 for sample Transcript Format

not always that simple. Transcripts are meant to be an exact rendering of the spoken word, but how exact do transcripts really need to be? There's no exact answer. Some oral historians opine that nothing less than every word, sound, and grammatical error should be included without omitting a single "um" or "hmm." These kinds of transcripts can be verrrrry long and sometimes hard to get through, but they are a great representation of the event. Others go so far as to correct grammatical errors in order to make the transcript more intelligible. Still others allow the narrator to review and edit their transcripts to ensure they are saying what they really want to say. This isn't a true transcript anymore as it doesn't mirror the primary source, but it can still be very useful. However you will go about it, make sure the interviewee understands your process and what will be expected of them before the interview.

While you may decide to omit false starts and "ums," you do not want to lose the pauses in the transcripts. Sometimes a break in speech can say as much as the words or add a new level of poignancy to them. Simply add [pause] in that segment. Similarly, include gestures and wordless reactions that add to the story. "I never thought about it until today. [Pauses for several minutes. Wipes away tears then smiles.] Thank you."

EDITING TRANSCRIPTS

"We make our interviews available by putting them up on our website. Technology helps get the stories out there instead of staying local to a particular community. We juxtapose text with video, showing clips instead of a whole interview.

"We decided not to give transcripts to the interviewees to edit. Often they can't decipher the rough draft and get angry at the mistakes. The transcript needs to be polished before showing it to them so we do a little editing. We will change verb tense only, not correct all the grammar."
—Project Director, *Telling Their Stories: Oral History Archives Project*

In general, the best rule of thumb is to go back to your project goals and think about where your transcripts will end up. If you are submitting the transcript to a library, find out what their requirements are before transcribing. Once your transcripts are made accessible, the information you provided will be reused over and over so be sure it is accurate. If you are interviewing people who might feel uncomfortable with their grammatical errors going on public record, consider cleaning them up. Legibility and usefulness are generally more important than exactitude.

Other Archiving Formats

If transcripts are too tall an order, consider creating an interview abstract or summary. An interview abstract summarizes the content of the interview, often in one hundred words or less. This method allows you to specify which topics you want to document instead of typing up every single word. For example, an interview summary could say: "Gordon spoke about his many jobs, one of which was beet farming. They used a really sharp curved tool to get beets out of the ground. One day he cut his knee with the tool and that was the end of his beet farming career."

Even if you transcribe your interviews, an interview summary can still be a very handy tool. Summaries can be utilized on websites, in catalogs, or for press releases, exhibition cases, and other public forums. Taking it one step further, you can create a very helpful guide for future transcribing by also typing up all names, tools, locations, and words that aren't immediately recognizable. If you decide not to record the interviews, consider writing up interview summaries that retell the narrator's stories without attempting to capture every word.

Another archiving format is the interview journal. Interviewers keep a journal to record not only what they heard but also what they learned and felt about the experience. Interviewers should make journal entries no more than twenty-four hours after each interview and can be assigned

AN ALTERNATIVE TO TRANSCRIPTS

"During the interview, the volunteer listens and jots down important information. The interviews are not recorded because this scares the residents. After the first interview, the volunteer goes home and types up what was shared. They write it up in first person and are not concerned about grammar—we want to hear the voice of the resident speaking. Then the volunteer makes a second appointment, comes back and reads the story back to the resident to make sure they got it correct. Nine out of ten times the resident says they forgot to tell them something or a date was wrong so generally there are edits to be done. The volunteer goes home and types up the notes. They set up a third appointment to ensure their edits are correct.

"Residents sign a permission form that says if they are willing to share their story or not. If not, the story is given to the resident to do whatever they want. We've collected 125 stories and only three haven't wanted to share the story.

We put the story in a nice plastic cover. The cover page has the name of the resident and their signature and any restrictions on who can read it. Stories are kept in our library where they are accessible to staff, residents, families or visitors—which is a nice way to promote the program. We make copies for families or friends, with the original going to the resident.

"I can't tell you how often they say, 'I don't have a story.' Then they do it and come up to you and say, 'Did you read my story?' It's a wonderful way of honoring the resident's life. It's a great way for staff to get a better insight into the resident. It helps us in getting them better care."

—Project Manager, *Life Storytelling Program*

specific questions to address in addition to general thoughts and impressions.

Many projects now also create websites to store and share their data. Websites are an excellent medium in terms of accessibility, with the added benefit of supporting two-way communication, but should not take the place of a more enduring archive. More ideas for sharing your project, such as exhibitions and public events, will be discussed in the next chapter.

ORAL HISTORY PACKAGE

In addition to the transcript itself, an archived oral history may include several other documents. Again, the purpose is to make the oral history as user-friendly as possible. Even if you don't plan on archiving your oral histories in a library, you may want to include other contextual documents to inform future users.

Your oral history package can include:
- Mission statement of sponsoring institution
- Project description
- Statement from project director, project manager, and/or interviewer(s)
- Supplemental documents that provide context to the interview, such as historical essays or time lines
- Bibliography
- List of other interviewees
- Transcript
- Photos, especially of the interviewer and interviewee together, with captions that say who is in the photo as well as where, when and by whom the photo was taken
- Newspaper clippings
- Letters or correspondence
- Interview recording(s)

The package can be presented in a variety of ways. Your main concern is that the packaging keep the materials safe and protected. Many stores now carry archival quality paper, folders, binders and adhesives. These archival products make a huge difference in the longevity of print materials, especially for newspapers and old documents and photos printed on highly acidic papers. Binding the materials together into a book assures that they'll remain together over the years. You can also put in a pocket or sleeve to hold CDs and DVDs.

You felt great when that interview was complete. It feels even better to have the whole package nice, neat and organized, ready for the world to see.

Other products

Transcripts, oral history packages, permanent archives—if all this is too much to think about, don't despair. Think of the many products that can come from your collection of oral histories, and start small. At the very least, you have some

EXCEEDING EXPECTATIONS

"We made audio recordings, about 5-8 minutes each. I had a connection with this incredible woman who produces radio shows. Radio felt more manageable than video since it's more low tech. Also, we don't have a computer lab. Radio production is cheaper than video production and it's easier to teach the kids to edit audio than video since I only have a few hours a month with them. The youth stories were never aired on public radio. They never got picked up but they're available through our website. Still, just knowing that they were producing for the radio was a big deal to the students. Knowing it was going out to the public really made them think: I never thought I'd have something to say on the radio! This sounded so serious, so far from where they could normally access. Suddenly the kids were in a league they didn't expect to be in.

"In a general way, the process of taking them seriously and believing what they have to say and what they've experienced really made them step up. They realized they'd better figure out what they really thought instead of just saying what everyone else was saying.

"Later, the museum we worked with added the students' stories to their audio tour. The kids were into that. Students want their voice to be heard. Knowing that there's a real place it's going is really meaningful."

—Project Director, *youTHink*

fantastic audio recordings, so make sure they are duplicated, labeled, and kept in a cool safe place. Same for video footage and all documents. The next step up might be to edit some of the audio and video footage into a compilation. Or, type up some of the stories and put together a simple book. It's becoming simpler to build websites these days to which you can very easily attach audio or video clips in addition to text and images.

Once your materials are properly documented and ready for preservation, you are ready to share your materials with the public. There are many ways—and reasons—to do this, as we'll discuss in the next chapter. As you'll see, integrating your materials into a final product and sharing it with others can increase the learning and take your project to a whole new level.

LESSONS LEARNED: ARCHIVING

Wish we had:
- Thought about archiving from the beginning. By the time we wrapped the interviews, we were out of time. Now all our CDs are just gathering dust in a desk drawer.
- Gotten the consent form signed before the interview. We couldn't get a hold of the interviewee afterwards, so we couldn't put his interview on the website with the others.
- Allotted enough time and money for transcribing. Luckily one of the volunteers really stepped up and took on most of the transcribing.

So glad we:
- Decided to record and film the interviews. An editor showed up at the last minute and made us a great highlight reel for our event.
- Partnered with a library. They helped us every step of the way and now people can actually use our interviews in their research.
- Took photos of each interviewer and interviewee. We didn't really know what we'd do with them but we've ended up using them a million ways, including on the covers of the oral history packages we put together for the local library.

CHAPTER SEVEN

Assimilation

"Our stories are the tellers of us."

—Chris Cleave

Chances are strong that months if not years have passed since the inception of your project. You have journeyed to places you never thought about before the project began. The stories of strangers are now stories of your own. Is this the end of the road?

Some projects will end at their appointed time. Others will find a new burst of life and continue to expand, often in unforeseen directions. Whichever way your project goes, you and your team will want closure before moving on. The step of assimilating achieves this closure by allowing time for reflection on what has been learned, sharing the project fruits with a larger audience, tying up loose ends, and cementing relationships.

REFLECTION

In an oral history interview, you are asking someone to look back at their life and not only describe events but reflect upon their meaning and significance. The same consideration is helpful for an oral history project itself. You've done a lot of work and amassed a lot of information. Young and old participants alike will appreciate the opportunity to look back on what they've gained and express it in their own way.

One way to assimilate the project is to invite your team to write an essay about their experience. Or, they can create an art project. These assignments can be done at home or you can create the time and space for them within the project structure itself. This step of reflection will implant participants' experiences and knowledge deeper into their memory banks. New understandings will undoubtedly flower as they approach the familiar material from a new angle. In addition to their memories, they will have something tangible to take with them when all is said and done.

PUTTING IT ALL TOGETHER

"Before the project I knew a little bit about my past but I wasn't as curious. It was not something I was interested in. I'm here now, and that's all that matters. I never thought about learning the history of my parents' country and what they went through... and how that defined them and then us.

"[For the project] we had to trace back our parents. We got ribbons and little tags and we tagged on a map where we are now, then back to where our father lived and put a tag on that exact location, and where our mother was born, and their parents and so on. We had a map on the wall and connected the ground our ancestors walked on.

"A lot of us didn't really know what to expect so we were shocked when the map was finished. We had to step back and just stare at it. We were surprised to see how long the strings went, how long was the journey of our grandparents and great grandparents and the journey of our bloodline. Some came from Asia, some from Germany, and now we are all here.

"A lot of people were very excited to learn about their history.... We had ancestors from different parts of the world we didn't expect, like we discovered that many of us have European blood.... Now I see everyone more as just people, and it made our past more connected with European past and the European past more connected to ours.

"I feel that it's important for Americans to understand the stories of other citizens because America is very diverse

Another simple approach to assimilation is to bring the youth together for a debrief session. The learning continues as they hear about the interviews they did not attend. The learning deepens as they discuss their experiences and what they appreciate about them. This is a good time to address any questions about the process or subject that may have come up over the course of the project. If you're planning future projects or phases, now is the time to invite involvement from this group of now-experienced—and invested—volunteers.

and [people] need to know that other people have very interesting stories and good reasons for why they came here. They came here to escape poverty and violence in their own county. I feel Americans need to know that we are diverse and we can be united and support one another. We are American, we are not a certain color or religion. We maintain our unity through telling stories. You are able to realize that a lot of people don't dislike you and you are able to connect more. Not a lot of people mean harm, they do their best. Sometimes people make the wrong decisions for the right reasons. You share stories and you see, this is another American and this is what they went through, so you don't feel far away from them, you feel close to them and you feel a part of history and can take that with you. We have more respect for each other and each other's culture and identity. We're able to connect with each other.

"It basically helps us respect each other. If there was any racism going around, through this project we were able to minimize that a little. When we told our stories, no one said anything bad. We listened to each other and what our parents went through and it wasn't a lie. It was the truth. When we spoke about our cultures, I didn't know that people from Nicaragua or Persia suffered discrimination as well. I didn't know that. I acknowledge that and can relate it to my own culture. Now, we as young people can pass the story down instead of it ending and no one can hear it."

—Youth Participant, *youTHink*

In addition to assimilation, this kind of finale program can be a chance to celebrate. Look at all you have accomplished! Give yourself the space to congratulate and thank one another for many jobs well done.

SHARING THE FRUITS

One of the precepts of oral history is to share what you have learned with the larger community. Many oral history grants require a culminating public exhibition or event, which also supports the oral historians' mission of making their work available and accessible. A bonus is that young people get really excited when their work goes public, be it speaking at an event or having their final project displayed in an art exhibit. A public finale can provide everyone with both motivation and a deadline, both of which can be very useful as a project rolls along.

Oral history presentations can take many forms. Again, much depends on your project goals, time line and budget. A community center with space for a public event will not need a big budget. If you don't have a space, this is another time to consider partnering with a community institution. For example, a library archiving your work may be interested in sponsoring an exhibition or public event to commemorate the addition of your work to their collection. All you need for an exhibition is a place to put stuff, and all you need for an event is a space, a speaker or two, and a simple event schedule. You can be as extravagant and creative as you like, but it doesn't have to be complicated.

Exhibitions

In the course of your project, you will have created and collected a number of stories and perhaps even photos, documents and other objects and products that can be curated into an intriguing, inspiring exhibit. Your audio and video recordings can be utilized in multi-media presentations. You can put together an edited product or play the interviews in their entirety. Photos and other artifacts can be matched with descriptive stories. You can also demonstrate the steps of your project and share any artwork or writing that has been created. For example, one school had the students create a ceramic sculpture to represent what they gained from their oral history experience. Their project culminated with a display of all their sculptures on family night.

In addition to showing what you have done, you can make it possible for others to experience a taste of oral history. Create interactive displays to allow visitors to share comments or their own stories. Make a little table with paper and crayons for children to draw their family tree. If your project has a geographical element, provide a large map of that area and make it possible for visitors to add their data. Provide questions and encourage visitors to ask their own families. These are just a few simple ideas to get you brainstorming.

Events

Everybody loves stories. They love to hear them, and they love to tell them. With this in mind, it's very easy to create an oral history event. You can put together a great event just by inviting the participants to speak about their experiences. Invite a few interviewees to share some great stories. Let the young people speak up as well. You can also invite stories from the audience. People may be interested in learning about the oral history process in general, or about the history of the area and events that your project uncovered. This is a perfect time to debut and sell the DVD you made or the book of stories you put together. It's also a good way to attract donors and continue to build community awareness and support. Again, the shape of your event will be determined by your goals. A fundraising event may look different from an art exhibit opening. Here is another opportunity to be creative! Oral history events have included not only art exhibits and storytelling but dance exhibitions and even food shows.

You can enlist support for your event or exhibition from your existing team. Find roles not only for the youth but also your community advisory team and interviewees. They can serve as ushers or guides for the exhibition in addition to speaking at the event. Have them available so people can talk to them and ask them questions one-on-one. This is their moment too.

Promoting your project

There's nothing like a public event to put your project on the map, or at least the social calendar. You've put in a lot of work, and you believe in your project. Still, you may be surprised by how many other people value it as well.

The core people most interested are the stakeholders in the theme being examined. For example, the Oakland Chinatown intergenerational oral history project culminated with a public event at the end of its first phase. This event attracted the people who lived there, especially elderly residents. It also attracted people whose family who came from that area as well as those who had experienced or were interested in the local history. People came because they wanted to compare the stories of this Chinatown with Chinatowns in another city, or because they were interested in Asian-American history. From students to journalists, immigrants to community members, everyone wanted to learn something that couldn't be found in the history books. Because the development of Chinatown has much in common with other immigrant communities and communities of color, the presentation attracted community activists and others involved with urban development. City officials showed up to make contact with their constituents. The event was covered in the local newspaper as well as three Chinese papers.

Even with such a large and varied potential audience, the key to promoting an oral history project is still word of mouth. Staff, advisors, project participants and their families —these are the ones who will bring people to your event. In addition, send invites to everyone on your contact list. You might be surprised by who is interested so don't be afraid to cast your net wide. If you have media contacts, use them. Send out a general media press release. Get a sound bite on the local radio station or cable network. Promotion can be time consuming; put together a time line so you are sure to contact the right people at the right time.

VIDEO RELEASE PARTY

"[A team of people] compiled all the videos of our interviews and they edited it into a DVD. They broke it into sections, but really it was a collection of different parts of our stories so you could see what was different and what was similar over the years. I remember when they finally finished the film. We had a showing at the library. It was really neat to see how the stories blended together. I liked seeing the contrast between the stories. One of the juniors had talked about her iPod and music, whereas Gordon had only one radio in the whole town and their entertainment was going out to look at the wild horses or going to the home of the man on the unpaved main street of town who was known as the local windbag, so people would go listen to him if they wanted entertainment.

"I thought that was really cool the way they made the video. It was interesting to see how they put which pieces where, and to see what the other people said."

—Youth Participant, *Fusing Identities*

BUILDING BRIDGES

To some extent, every oral history project is a community endeavor. In addition to documenting and preserving history, you are also creating relationships that can be meaningful long after a project is complete. To ensure this connection lasts, take the time to acknowledge everyone on your extended team and communicate where you'd like to go from here.

It's also never too late for feedback. Let your community team know that everything is wrapped up and ask them where they'd like the project to go next. One project director was planning to end the project until the community team provided both momentum and resources to keep it going; the project is now in its fifth year. Regardless of whether the project is perpetuated, you still want to elicit feedback from your team. Not only will this support your learning and any future projects, it also conveys respect to the people who have helped make your project a success.

The same is true with community partners. In addition to expressing gratitude, let them know all the products and results of the project and where they can be accessed. Share any plans or ideas for the future—especially if you're hoping they will continue to work with you. Assuming a healthy, trusting relationship has been built, this is also a time to look back on what worked and what could be improved within your partnerships. By taking the time to consider and communicate these learning lessons, you improve your own methodology and help your partners do the same. Whether you have concrete plans for the future or not, wrap up in a way that leaves the door open for future collaboration.

SHARING LEARNING LESSONS

"After partnering with another oral history project for our second phase, I had a great meeting with the woman I'd been collaborating with. We talked about what we had learned through this process. I expressed how great it was that they could provide us with time, personnel, and equipment to record stories at no cost to us. She asked me if there was anything we could have done to improve the partnership. Before this conversation, she and I had many many conversations so we already had a trusting relationship and were ready to be open with each other about things that could have gone better. I told her that I'd had a difficult time understanding their guidelines for community partnership. She acknowledged the need to set up a better infrastructure for this, especially when they are going into new areas. We had just been making it up as we went along and now I like to think that this has helped them and the communities they'll be supporting in the future."
—Project Director, *Oakland Chinatown Oral History Project*

Even if you feel complete with your project, there may be others in the local area or global community who could benefit from your stories or process. Oral history symposiums

TAKING YOUR PROJECT ON THE ROAD

"A school in Mississippi found out about our project and was interested in doing something similar. I actually flew out there on my vacation time to help them. The school was in a very poor community, where most of the students feel they have no future if they don't make it to college. I loved to watch the kids getting blown away by the experience. One of the interviews actually became a community event with many people dropping by to watch or listen…. A story about their project even made the front page of local newspaper. [Participating in the project] showed the students that they do have power. They have the potential to have an impact on their community."

—Project Director, *Telling Their Stories: Oral History Archives Project*

and conferences are an excellent place to share your project and learn more about others doing similar projects around the world. Schools can also reach out to other schools and teachers to let them know how they made the project work. In many cases, it is easier to replicate a process than create one from scratch. There may be a school or museum that would love to pick up where you left off.

Oral history and community activism

Another area where oral history can play a big role is community activism. In order for community activism to be successful, you need historical information. You need to know the past in order to inform the future. As Harvard professor Howard Gardner says, "Stories are the single most powerful weapon in a leader's arsenal."

Activism exists in the first place because the community feels that it has been wronged. How it has been wronged needs to be documented. You can't approach a government institution to say, "We've been wronged," if you have no information and proof to give them. With proof you can formulate a complete argument for the community future you are trying to advocate for. This angle may also provide a compelling reason for potential narrators to share their stories. Wanting to preserve stories may not be reason enough, but they may open up if their experience can help bring about positive change.

ACTIVISM AND ORAL HISTORY

"For some people, it's often not enough to say you want their story because you want it to be documented. In general, unless you are famous, no one is approaching you to document your history and even if they did, you don't think it's interesting or important anyway. There are other reasons. Collecting stories so apartheid won't happen again. So there will not be another Pol Pot in Cambodia. So Chinatown will not be wiped out again in the next urban renewal."

—Project Director, *Oakland Chinatown Oral History Project*

WRAP UP THE DETAILS

When all is said and done, inevitably there are still a few things left to say and do. Now is the time to make sure no details, such as thank you cards, have fallen through the cracks. It's also important to document your work in such a way that it can be picked back up by a new team in the future, should the opportunity arise.

An excellent way to document your own process for posterity is to create a manual of your process. This will not only help the next team pick up where you left off but also serves as a central organizing place for all the materials generated by the project, from forms to question lists, brochures to photographs.[23] As we've seen, the human memory is very selective. Even if you've been intimately involved with every detail of the project, it's amazing how much you'll forget in a year's time. In addition, the creation of a manual can lend extra credibility to your project. This kind

---

23. See Appendix 13 for sample Manual Contents

of documentation shows how much you value the project. It's fairly simple to create something very professional that you can show to others years after the project has ended. Think of a manual as your own version of this book—everything you did to make the process happen. Creating a manual also can provide good physical and emotional closure for people involved with the project. Even if you are moving on to further phases, the creation and presentation of a manual signifies that this portion of your project is complete.

Before you close the book on your project, you will also want to check the status of your archiving. For example, if you have provided transcripts to a library, find out how they are coming along with the finished archival product. If you are doing your own archiving, ensure that everything is clearly labeled and in a safe, organized place. Check your digital storage as well the hard copies. Designate a person to maintain oversight of the archiving process and collection so they can keep the team updated as necessary.

If you've had an exhibition or collected artifacts, be sure to have a plan for returning materials once the exhibition is finished. Again, designating a specific person for this task can make this easier for everyone.

Finally, take the time to fully acknowledge your team. Everyone who helped in any way—from volunteers to major sponsors to the café that provided free coffee for your event —deserves recognition as well as information about where things will go from here. If applicable, encourage student volunteers to seek community service units or extra credit for their participation and find out how you can help.

LESSONS LEARNED: ASSIMILATION

Wish we had...
- Planned more debrief time with the students. After the interviews, everyone kind of went their own way and we were never able to get them all together again.
- Started promoting our event sooner. By the time we got around to it, the event was only a few weeks away and the attendance was not as high as we'd hoped.
- Stayed in touch with a radio producer who wanted to do a radio show about our program. By the time we realized the value of her offer, it was too late.

So glad we:
- Put together a little exhibit. We were very surprised by the great reactions we got from those who attended, and it allowed the parents to see what their kids had been up to all this time.
- Invited a few of the youth interviewers to speak at the event. The audience was just as moved by their words as they were by the interviewees' stories. I suspect this element led to some of the more generous financial donations.
- Kept in touch with our community team, even after the project was "complete". Now we are in a second phase and they are all on board!
- Invited the students to act as guides for the exhibit. They were nervous at first but really loved being able to talk to others about the project and what they'd learned.

EVERYONE WINS

All the details have been attended to. Everyone on your extended team feels thanked and knows where to find the products created in your work together. Future plans are clear yet there is a satisfying sense of closure. Now it is really time to celebrate.

This book is filled with true stories of people and communities that have benefited from oral history, yet only a tiny number of such projects are represented here. Thanks to the great efforts of oral historians, both new and established, and forward thinking teachers, grant agencies, community leaders and many others, new projects continue to spring up all the time around the world.

As we've seen, the benefit continues long after the project is finished. Young people become more interested in history. They are eager to learn where they came from and feel more comfortable and enthusiastic about talking to elders and their own family. Elders are able to pass on their cultural legacy and take comfort in the expression of who they are. Individuals and communities learn to respect one another for their similarities and differences alike. Story bridges reconnect segmented families, communities and societies for generations to come.

In the words of a Siberian elder, "If you don't know the trees you may be lost in the forest, but if you don't know the stories you may be lost in life." Story bridges will always bring you home.

APPENDIX

Appendix Contents

APPENDIX 1: Sample Mission Statements

The Oakland Chinatown Oral History Project (OCOHP), spearheaded by the Oakland Asian Cultural Center (OACC), aims to capture the living history of Oakland Chinatown by bringing youth to interview Oakland Chinatown elders. The goals of the OCOHP are to document the stories of Oakland Chinatown, preserve its cultural and historical legacy, and increase understanding across generations.

—Oakland Chinatown Oral History Project

Students gain deep understanding of modern history through face-to-face involvement documenting the stories of our elders, while at the same time providing a public service via the publication of their interviews. The course serves to expand the [school's] study of the diverse Bay Area history while directly addressing part of the school mission of extending our reach to the community "by meaningful engagement with the real world outside the classroom."

—Oral History Archives Project

APPENDIX 2: Sample Oral History Project Budget

Budget Item	Item Cost
Project Manager salary, $50/hour for 60 hours	$3,000
Audio editor/technician	$1,500
Interview transcription, 100 hours at $30/hour	$3,000
Honoraria for two humanities scholars (historian, oral historian) at $350 each	$700
Interview travel and meal expenses for volunteers	$500
Audio equipment purchase – 2 digital recorders at $250 each + 2 exterior mics at $200 each + tax	$1,000
CDs, batteries, and cables	$150
External hard drive for file storage	$100
Office supplies	$100
Photocopies for flyers, brochures, etc.	$250
Research materials	$300
Publicity and marketing	$500
Rental fee for event space	$600
Refreshments for event	$250
Honoraria for guest speakers – 2 at $150 each	$300
Exhibition costs (printing, etc.)	$750
Misc. expenses	$500
Total	$13,500

APPENDIX 3: Consent Form

Name of Organization

Address, Telephone Numbers, Email addresses

Release Form

Thank you for participating in the *[name of project]*. Please read and sign this form to give us permission to share your words and images in [name of project's] publications/photographs/videos/websites.

By signing this form, I give consent to [project name] to use, exhibit, publish, and reproduce my name, image, likeness, and statements in [project name]publications/photographs/videos/websites.

By signing this form, I also release [project name] from any liability based on the use of my name, image, likeness and statements, including for example, any claim based on defamation, rights of publicity, or invasion of privacy. Likewise, I also release all affiliated partners, including their individual employees, supervisors, and participants from liability.

I acknowledge that the [project name] will rely on this consent and release in producing, broadcasting and distributing programs and works.

I understand that I will receive no monetary compensation for giving this consent and release. Likewise, the [project name] is under no obligation to make the use of these materials.

I understand that photographic and video documentation will be involved and consent to having pictures of me taken. This material may be used for the [project name] and its partner's publication, events, educational materials, websites and broadcasts. It may be used for commercial purposes.

_____   _____

PARTICIPANT NAME (PRINT)   **SIGNATURE and DATE**

_____

ADDRESS

_____

PHONE/EMAIL

APPENDIX 4: Consent Form for Minors

Name of Organization

Address, Telephone Numbers,
Email addresses

Release Form for Minors

Thank you for participating in the *[name of project]*. Please read and sign this form to give us permission to share your words and images in [name of project's] publications/photographs/videos/websites.

By signing this form, I give consent to [project name] to use, exhibit, publish, and reproduce my name, image, likeness, and statements in [project name]publications/photographs/videos/websites.

By signing this form, I also release [project name] from any liability based on the use of my name, image, likeness and statements, including for example, any claim based on defamation, rights of publicity, or invasion of privacy. Likewise, I also release all affiliated partners, including their individual employees, supervisors, and participants from liability.

I acknowledge that the [project name] will rely on this consent and release in producing, broadcasting and distributing programs and works.

I understand that I will receive no monetary compensation for giving this consent and release. Likewise, the [project name] is under no obligation to make the use of these materials.

I understand that photographic and video documentation will be involved and consent to having pictures of me taken. This material may be used for the [project name] and its partner's publication, events, educational materials, websites and broadcasts. It may be used for commercial purposes.

_____   _____
PARTICIPANT NAME (PRINT)   SIGNATURE and DATE

_____   _____
LEGAL GUARDIAN NAME (PRINT)   SIGNATURE and DATE

_____
ADDRESS

_____
PHONE/EMAIL

APPENDIX 5: Acquired Objects Form

Name of Organization

Address, Telephone Numbers, Email addresses

Acquired Objects Form

Borrowed materials (include condition of materials with description)

    1. _____

    2. _____

    3. _____

    4. _____

Conditions for Use

    1. _____

    2. _____

    3. _____

    4. _____

Conditions for Storage

    1. _____

    2. _____

    3. _____

Date for return of materials: _____

Materials to be returned via:

    ☐ Picked up by lender

    ☐ Returned to home of lender by borrower

    ☐ Other (please specify) _____

Signature of Lender: _____

Type or print name: _____

Date: _____

Address: _____

Email: _____

Signature of Borrower: _____

Type or print name: _____

Date: _____

Address: _____

Email: _____

<u>APPENDIX 6: Recruitment Event Schedule</u>

Goals
- Inspire youth to participate in a valuable learning experience that supports the community
- Inform youth about the benefits of participating (Historical value, school credit, Interviewing skills, etc.)
- Clarify essential information (meeting times, contact information, how to get involved)

Schedule
5:00   Welcome, Introduce team, context presentation
5:05   Explain project, mission, and what the youth will be doing
5:10   Explain the benefits of their participation
5:15   Personal share of youth interviewer
5:17   Q & A; pass around sign-up sheet; hand out packets
5:20   Presentation ends

Youth Recruitment Packet
1. Flyer about project and the benefits of volunteering for this project
2. Next steps: an outline of what they will be experiencing
3. Meeting schedule and/or project time line
4. Information about the final event/exhibit/project
5. Information about how to get school credit
6. List of sponsoring institutions
7. Contact information for their designated contact person

APPENDIX 7: Volunteer Training Schedule

[Project Name] Youth Interviewer Workshop
Saturday June 11, 2:00 - 4:30

Workshop Goals
Workshop participants will:
- Connect with the other team members and their reasons for joining the project
- Learn basic oral history and interviewing skills and feel confident about their role as interviewers
- Understand the next steps in the [project name] process

Handouts
1. Project mission statement and goals
2. Personal goals statement
3. Oral History Guidelines
4. Interview question formats
5. Interview Question list
6. Interview Tips
7. Consent form

Workshop schedule

2:00   **Youth Liaison:** Welcome, intro Project Director

2:02   **Project Director:** Brief history of project and sponsoring institution(s); Mission statement (Handout #1)

2:05   **Youth Liaison:** Introduction Circle—Name, school, role in project, why you joined team

2:15   What are your personal goals for this project? Write them down (Handout #2) and Share (time permitting)

2:20   **Youth interviewers:** Personal experience of their participation; View video clip from previous interview

2:25   **Module One: Oral history guidelines**
General guidelines for conducting an oral history project (Handout #3)

2:35   Module Two: Interview Questions
Sample questions + question formats (Handout #4)

2:45   Break (Make copies of personal goal handouts)

2:50   Interview questions (Handout #5)
Review list of general questions, add their own questions to the list and share with group

3:10   Module Three: Interview Process
Clarify details such as: scheduling meetings with the interviewee, signing forms, room set up, equipment usage, how to document artifacts, archiving plan, etc.

3:15   Module Three: Interviewing Tips (Handout #6)

3:20   Practice interviews

3:40   Break

3:50   Live interviews with feedback from group

4:10   Q & A
Remind them to contact liaison with any questions, any time!

4:20   Set up interviews and other meetings
When are you available? Are you around this summer?

4:25   Next Steps and Expectations
Discuss upcoming meetings, research and pre-interview preparation. Speak about what you expect from volunteers, such as arriving on time, dressing appropriately, how to make a schedule change, etc.

4:30   Sign Release Form (Handout #7)

4:30   Workshop ends*

---

* Note: Make time for equipment training in this training or another session as needed

APPENDIX 8: Pre-Interview Worksheet

Your name: _____

Name of interviewee(s): _____

Interview Date: _____

Interview Location: _____

Interview topics: _____

Consent form signed? _____

Does interviewee understand how this recording will be used?

Biographical information

Date of birth: _____

Location of birth: _____

Nationality: _____

Places lived: _____

Married? If yes, when and where? _____

Children: _____

Education: _____

Work experience: _____

Personal experience (honors, awards, group affiliations, hobbies, etc.): _____

Information about family (parents' or other relatives' names, places of birth, careers):

_____

_____

_____

Focal point of interview: dates, events, locations, etc.

_____

_____

_____

Preliminary Questions:

_____

_____

_____

APPENDIX 9: Post-Interview Question List

- How did your interview go?
- What was easy?
- What was difficult?
- How could you have been better prepared?
- What did you learn from the interview?
- What did you learn about [project focus]?
- What did you learn about history and/or culture?
- What did you learn about yourself?
- What would you like to learn more about?
- What story had the most impact on you?
- What emotions did you feel upon hearing these stories?
- Did anything relate to your own experiences or your family's experiences? Please elaborate.
- Did anything surprise you?
- Did the interview meet your expectation? Please elaborate.
- What were your personal goals for this project?
- How have you met them?
- What more would you like to do to meet these goals?
- Do you have new goals now that you've done this interview? What are they?
- How has the interview changed or enlightened your perspective about elders?
- How has this interview changed or enlightened your perspective about [project focus]?
- What are the benefits of this kind of project?
- For yourself?
- For the community?
- For the world?
- What would you like to say to the other youth interviewers after your experience today?
- What would you like to say to the elder you interviewed?
- What kind of elder would you like to be?

APPENDIX 10: Oral History Data Template

(To be completed by oral history project for each interview. Pay attention to correct spelling of all names and places)

Narrator's full name and year of birth _____
Interviewer's full name and year of birth _____
Names and functions of other people involved (e.g. videographer).

_____ _____

Preferred title for interview (common title is [First name, last name] oral history] _____
Date and place of interview: _____
Title of oral history project _____
Sponsoring institution(s) _____
Specify additional or related interviews _____

_____

Biographical summary (no more than 150 words):

_____
_____
_____
_____

Interview summary (no more than 150 words): _____

_____
_____
_____
_____

Historical context (no more than 150 words): _____

_____
_____
_____
_____

Keywords associated with interview (Include personal and institutional names, place names, and topics) _____

_____
_____
_____

Accompanying materials (photos, clippings, documents) _____

_____
_____
_____

APPENDIX 11: Oral History Programs List

Colleges and Universities

- Baylor University Institute for Oral History, www.baylor.edu/Oral History/
- University of California at Berkeley Regional Oral History Office, bancroft.berkeley.edu/ROHO/
- University of Connecticut, Center for Oral History, www.oralhistory.uconn.edu/
- Indiana University Center for the Study of History and Memory, www.indiana.edu/~cshm/
- Marygrove College, John Novak Digital Interview Collection (Detroit, Michigan), lib.marygrove.edu/library/archives/oral_history/index.html
- Rutgers University, new Brunswick History Department, Oral History Archives, oralhistory.rutgers.edu/
- Southern Oral History Program, The University of North Carolina at Chapel Hill, Center for the Study of the American South, www.sohp.org/
- University of Southern Mississippi Center for Oral History and Cultural Heritage, www.usm.edu/oralhistory/
- University of Texas at El Paso Institute of Oral History, academics.utep.edu/Default.aspx?alias+academics.utep.edu/oralhistory
- Tulane University, Hogan Jazz Archive, www.tulane.edu/~lmiller/JazzHome.html
- Yale University – Oral History, American Music, www.yale.edu.oham/

Government Programs

- Archives of American Art, Smithsonian Institution, www.aaa.si.edu/
- California State Oral History Program, www.sos.ca.gov/archives/oral-history

- National Air and Space Museum, Department of Space History, www.nasm.si.edu/research/dsh/ohp-introduction.html
- The Library of Congress, American Memory, memory.loc.gov/ammem/index.html
- Social Security Administration, Oral History Collection, www.ssa.gov/history/orallist.html
- Veteran's History Project, Library of Congress, American Folklife Center, www.loc.gov/vets/

Other programs

- D.C. Everest Area Schools Oral History Program, www.dce.k12.wi.us/srhigh/socialstudies/histday/
- Densho: The Japanese American Legacy Project, www.densho.org/
- The Maria Rogers Oral History Program, Carnegie Branch Library for Local History, boulderlibrary.org/oralhistory/
- Museum of Performance and Design, Legacy Oral History Program, www.muse-sf.org/legacy.html
- StoryCorps, storycorps.org/

APPENDIX 12: Transcript Format*

Name of Project
Date of Interview
Location of Interview
Name of Interviewer(s)
Name of Interviewee(s)

Abbreviation for Interviewer [use initials, i.e., JS]
Abbreviation for Interviewee [LT]

JS: Tell me what it was like for you during the War.
LT: [Shrugs and laughs] Well, I don't remember much but what I do recall very clearly is the day that....

[Number all pages] 1

---

* For more examples, see the Baylor University Oral History Institute or the Maria Rogers Oral History Project websites

APPENDIX 13: Manual Contents

Introduction
- Sponsoring Institution
- Mission and Project Description
- Project Relevance
- Project Team

The Project
- Preparation
- Community Advisory Committee
- Define project goals
- Selecting interviewees
- Recruiting youth interviewers
- Developing interview questions
- Youth Interview Workshop
- Create Interview Teams
- Interview process
- Pre-interview meeting
- Interview—Day of, preparation
- Conducting interview
- Post-interview
- Field trip
- Interview Transcripts
- Archives
- Public Event
- Exhibit
- Community and Media Outreach
- Youth Engagement
- Wrap-Up
- Learning Lessons

Appendixes
1. Project Resource List—Books, films, websites, etc.
2. Consent Form
3. Youth Recruitment Flyer
4. Youth Recruitment Presentation materials
5. Interview Questions, general template

6. Interview Questions, customized list
7. Youth Interview Workshop Schedule
8. Youth Interview Workshop handout
9. Post-Interview Questions
10. Public event schedule and materials
11. Project brochure
12. Suggestion Form
13. Agreement to Loan form
14. Press Release
15. Public Service Announcement
16. Newspaper articles about Project
17. Project event flyer (with event date)
18. Sample Thank you letter
19. List of all items in Project Collection

APPENDIX 14: Oral History Resource List*

ORAL HISTORY

- Baum, Willa K. *Oral history for the local historical society.* 3rd ed. (Altamira Press, 1995).
- Charlton, Thomas L., Lois E. Myers, and M. Rebecca Sharpless, eds. *Handbook of oral history.* (AltaMira Press, 2006).
- Dunaway, David K. and Willa K. Baum, eds. *Oral history: an interdisciplinary anthology.* 2d ed. (AltaMira Press, 1996).
- Frisch, Michael. *A shared authority: essays on the craft and meaning of oral history and public history.* (State University of New York Press, 1990).
- *H-NET* (Online community). Interdisciplinary community of scholars and educators in the humanities and social sciences. Supports online discussion groups in specialized areas, including the ones mentioned below. www.h-net.org
- *H-ORALHIST* (Online discussion group). Moderated H-Net discussion group serves the oral history community. Subscription information and archives at www.h-net.org/~oralhist/
- *H-PUBLIC* (Online discussion group). Moderated H-Net discussion group for public history. Subscription information and archives at www.h-net.org/~public
- Lanman, Barry A. and Laura M. Wending, eds. *Preparing the next generation of oral historians: an anthology of oral history education.* (AltaMira Press, 2006).
- Linehan, Andy, ed. *Aural history: essays on recorded sound.* (British Library, National Sound Archive, 2001) Book plus CD. Published on the occasion International Association of Sound and Audiovisual Archives Conference.
- Oral History Association. *Evaluations guidelines.* www.dickinson.edu/oha/pub_eg.html.

---

* This list is also available online at www.nancymackay.net/curating/resources.htm

- Perks, Robert and Alistair Thomson, eds. *The oral history reader.* 2nd ed. (Routledge, 2006).
- Portelli, Alessandro. *The battle of Valle Giulia: oral history and the art of dialogue.* (University of Wisconsin Press, 1997). -

----. *The death of Luigi Trastulli and other stories : form and meaning in oral history.* (State University of New York Press, 1991).

----. *The order has been carried out: history, memory and meaning of a Nazi massacre in Rome.* (Palgrave Macmillan, 2003).

- Ritchie, Donald A. *Doing oral history : a practical guide.* 2nd ed. (Oxford University Press, 2003).
- Schneider, William. *So they understand: cultural issues in oral history.* (Utah State University Press, 2002)
- Sommer, Barbara W. and Mary Kay Quinlan. *The oral history manual.* (AltaMira Press, 2002).
- Thompson, Paul. *The voice of the past: oral history.* 3rd ed. (Oxford University Press, 2000).
- Whitman, Glenn. *Dialogue with the past: engaging students & meeting standards through oral history.* (AltaMira Press, 2004).
- Yow, Valerie Raleigh. *Recording oral history; a guide for the humanities and social sciences.* 2d. ed. (AltaMira Press, 2005).

ARCHIVES ADMINISTRATION

- *Archives and Archivists Listserv* (Online discussion group). Unmoderated, high volume forum for archivists. Archives available. Subscribe at listserv.muohio.edu/archives/archives.html
- ARMA International and Society of American Archivists. *Sample forms for archival and records management programs.* (ARMA, SAA, 2002). Forms in electronic format can be copied from accompanying CD.
- Bradsher, James Gregory. *Managing archives and archival institutions.* (University of Chicago Press, 1991)
- Carmicheal, David W. *Organizing archival records: a*

practical method of arrangement & description for small archives. 2nd ed. (AltaMira Press, 2005).

- Danielson, Virginia, Elizabeth Cohen and Anthony Seeger. *Folk heritage collections in crisis.* (CLIR, 2001) Papers from a 2000 conference on the condition of heritage collections. www.clir.org/pubs/reports/pub96/contents.html
- Farrington, Jim. *Audio and video equipment basics for libraries.* (Scarecrow Press, 2006).
- Fox, Michael J., Peter Wilkerson, and Suzanne Warren. *Introduction to archival organization and description: access to cultural heritage.* (Getty Information Institute, 1999). www.getty.edu/research/conducting_research/standards/introarchives
- *NINCH guide to good practice in the digital representation and management of cultural heritage materials.* (NINCH, 2002). www.nyu.edu/its/humanities/ninchguide
- Hunter, Gregory S. *Developing and maintaining practical archives: a how-to-do-it manual.* 2nd ed. (Neal-Schuman, 2003).
- International Council on Archives. *General International Standard Archival Description (ISAD(G)).* 2nd ed. (International Council on Archives, 2000). www.ica.org/biblio/cds/isad_g_2e.pdf
- Kurtz, Michael. *Managing archival and manuscript repositories.* (Society of American Archivists, 2004).
- Pearce-Moses, Richard. *Glossary of archival and records terminology.* (Society of American Archivists, 2005). www.archivists.org/glossary
- Roe, Kathleen D. *Arranging & describing archives & manuscripts.* (Society of American Archivists, 2005). Supercedes Frederic Miller's *Arranging and describing archives and manuscripts* (1990).
- Society of American Archivists. *Describing archives: a content standard (DACS).* (Society of American Archivists, 2004.) Revised standard for archival description. Supercedes Steven Hensen's *Archives, personal papers and manuscripts* (1989).

- ---. *A guide to deeds of gift.* (Society of American Archivists, 1998). www.archivists.org/publications/deed_of_gift.asp
- Stielow, Frederick J. *The management of oral history sound archives.* (Greenwood Press, 1986).
- Swain, Ellen D. "Oral history in the archives: it's documentary role in the twenty-first century," *American Archivist*, v. 66 (Spring/summer 2003): 139-158.
- Walch, Victoria Irons, comp. *Standards for archival description : a handbook.* (Society of American Archivists, 1994) Online version by Stephen Miller. www.archivists.org/catalog/stds99/index.html
- Ward, Alan. *A manual of sound archive administration.* (Gower Publishing Company, 1990).
- Wilsted, Thomas and William Nolte. *Managing archival and manuscript repositories.* (Society of American Archivists, 1991).
- Yakel, Elizabeth. *Starting an archives.* (Society of American Archivists, Scarecrow Press, 1994).

LEGAL & ETHICAL ISSUES

- Benedict, Karen. *Ethics and the archival profession: introduction and case studies.* (Society of American Archivists, 2003) Forty case studies covering all aspects of archival management.
- Brown, Michael F. "Can culture be copyrighted?" *Current Anthropology.* Vol.39, No.2 (April 1998): 193-222.
- *Copyright Resources Project : working with copyrighted materials in a digital environment* (University of California Art Museum & Pacific Film Archive, 2005). www.bampfa.berkeley.edu/pfa_library/copyright_project
- *Digital Millennium Copyright Act (DMCA).* Government summary of the legislation: www.copyright.gov/legislation/dmca.pdf For a summary and interpretation from the UCLA Institute for Cyberspace Law and Policy, see www.gseis.ucla.edu/iclp/dmca1.htm
- *Fair Use in the Electronic Age*, compiled by American Association of Law Libraries, American Library

Association, Association of Academic Health Sciences Library Directors, Association of Research Libraries, Medical Library Association, and Special Libraries Association. www.arl.org/info/frn/copy/fairuse.html

- Lipinski, Thomas A., ed. *Libraries, museums and archives: legal issues and ethical challenges in the new Information Age.* (Scarecrow Press, 2002).
- Neuenschwander, John A. *Oral history and the law.* 3rd ed. (Oral History Association, 2002). Acknowledged authority among oral historians for legal issues in oral history.
- Padfield, Tim. *Copyright for archivists and users of archives.* 2d ed. (Facet, 2004). Copyright issues in the United Kingdom.
- Russell, Carrie. *Complete copyright: an everyday guide for librarians.* (American Library Association, 2004).
- Schneider, William. *So they understand : cultural issues in oral history.* (Utah State University Press, 2002). Ethical issues in oral history.
- Society of American Archivists. *A guide to deeds of gift.* (Society of American Archivists, 1998). www.archivists.org/publications/deed_of_gift.asp
- Stim, Richard. *Getting permission: how to license & clear copyrighted materials online & off.* (Nolo Press, 2004).
- United States Copyright Office. *Report on orphan works.* (United States Copyright Office, Library of Congress, 2006). www.copyright.gov/orphan/orphan-report-full.pdf
- University of Texas. *Fair use of copyrighted works.* Sample interpretation of fair use. www.utsystem.edu/OGC/intellectualProperty/copypol2.htm

PROFESSIONAL ETHICAL STANDARDS

- Alaska Native Knowledge Network. *Guidelines for respecting cultural knowledge.* Adopted 2000. www.ankn.uaf.edu/publications/knowledge.html
- American Anthropological Association. *Statements on ethics.* Rev. 1986. www.aaanet.org/stmts/stmts/ethstmnt.htm

- American Association of State and Local History. *Statement of professional standards and ethics.* Rev. 2002. www.aaslh.org/ethics.htm
- American Association of Museums. *Code of ethics for museums.* Rev. 2000. www.aam-us.org/museumresources/ethics/coe.cfm
- American Historical Association. *Statement on standards of professional conduct.* Rev. 2005. www.historians.org/pubs/Free/ProfessionalStandards.cfm
- American Library Association. *Code of ethics.* www.ala.org/ala/oif/statementspols/codeofethics/codeethics.htm
- Oral History Association. *Evaluation Guidelines.* Rev. 2000. omega.dickinson.edu/organizations/oha/pub_eg.html
- Society of American Archivists. *Code of ethics for archivists.* Rev. 2005. www.archivists.org/governance/handbook/app_ethics.asp

RECORDING TECHNOLOGY

- *AMIL-L: Online forum for moving image archivists.* Subscription information and archives at www.amianet.org/amial/amial.html
- *ARSC recorded round discussion list.* Unmoderated discussion list for sound recording discussions at all levels. Subscription information at www.arsc-audio.org/arsclist.html
- Bennett, Hugh. *Understanding CD-R and CD-RW: physical, logical and file system standards.* (Optical Storage Technology Association, 2003). www.osta.org/technology/pdf/cdr_cdrw.pdf
- *DAT-Heads: Digital Audio Tape.* Online discussion group for digital audio tape. www.solorb.com/dat-heads
- Hess, Richard. *Media formats and resources.* Demystifies recording formats. richardhess.com/notes/formats
- Historical Voices. *Oral history tutorial: audio technology.* (MATRIX (Michigan State University), 2002). www.historicalvoices.org/oralhistory/audio-tech.html

- Kovolos, Andy. *Audio field recording equipment guide.* (Vermont Folklife Center, frequent updates). The latest information on audio technology specifically for oral historians. www.vermontfolklifecenter.org/res_audioequip.htm
- Magnetic Reference Laboratory. *MRL homepage.* (Magnetic Reference Laboratory, frequently updated). Everything about magnetic tape. home.flash.net/~mrltapes
- *Minidisc.org.* Everything about minidiscs. www.minidiscorg
- Morton, David L. *History of sound recording technology.* (2003). www.recording-history.org
- ---- *Sound recording: the life story of a technology.* (Johns Hopkins University, 2006).
- ProAction Media. *Online glossary of CD/DVD terms.* (ProAction Media, 2005). www.proactionmedia.com/cd_dvd_glossary.htm
- Robbins, Ryan. *The Holy Grail of digital recording.* (Tape Transcription Center, n.d.). www.tctranscriptions.com/DigitalRecordingHolyGrail.html
- Schoenherr, Steve. *Recording technology history.* (2005). Timeline for recording technology. history.acusd.edu/gen/recording/notes.html
- Schouhamer Immink, Kees A. "The compact disc story." *Journal of Audio Engineering Society*, v.46, no.5 (May 1998). www.exp-math.uni-essen.de/~immink/pdf/cdstory.pdf
- Smolian, Steve. *SoundSaver.com: CDs from old recordings.* (SoundSaver.com, frequently updated.) Overview of older recording technology. soundsaver.com
- Tape Transcription Center. *Digital recording: here to stay.* (Tape Transcription Center, 2006). www.ttctranscriptions.com/Digitalvsanalog.html
- Taylor, Jim. *DVD demystified.* 3rd ed. (McGraw-Hill, 2006). A lot of information on accompanying website www.dvddemystified.com
- *Transom.org.* (Atlantic Public Media, frequently updated).

Easy to understand tips on recording technology. www. transom.org/tools

- UCSC Electronic Music Studios. *EMS equipment documents*. (University of California, Santa Cruz, Music Dept., content frequently updated). Technical articles on recording technology, with illustrations. arts.ucsc.edu/ ems/music/equipment/equipment.html
- *Wikipedia* has a variety of articles with helpful links on recording technology. en.wikipedia.org

TRANSCRIBING

- Baum, Willa K. *Transcribing and editing oral history*. (Altamira Press, 1995).
- Frisch, Michael. "Oral history and the digital revolution: toward a post-documentary sensibility." In *The oral history reader*. 2nd ed., Robert Perks and Alistair Thomson, eds. (Routledge, 2006). A case for alternatives to transcribing.
- Klemmer, Scott R. et al. *"Books with voices: paper transcripts as a physical interface to oral histories."* In *Proceedings of the SIGCHI conference on human factors in computer systems*, **2003. 89-96.**
- Powers, Willow Roberts. *Transcription techniques for the spoken word*. (AltaMira Press, 2005).
- University of Chicago Press. *Chicago manual of style*. 15th ed. (University of Chicago Press, 2003). Accepted standard among oral historians for usage, editing, and proofreading.
- Wilmsen, Carl. "For the record: editing and the production of meaning in oral history." *Oral history review*. 28:1 (Winter 2001).

TRANSCRIPTION SOFTWARE

- *Express-scribe transcription playback software*. (NCH Swift Sound). Free software for transcribing from digital files. www.nch.com.au/scribe
- *Start-stop dictation and transcription systems*. (HTH Engineering). Software for transcribing from digital files. www.startstop.com

TRANSCRIBING & EDITING GUIDES

- Minnesota Historical Society Oral History Office. *Transcribing, editing and processing oral histories.* (Oral History Association of Minnesota, 1996). www.oham. org/how/transcribe.html
- Baylor University Institute for Oral History. *Style guide: a quick guide for editing oral memoirs.* Rev. 2005. www. baylor.edu/oral%5fhistory/pdf/styleguide.pdf

CATALOGING

- American Library Association. *Anglo-American Cataloging Rules.* 2nd ed. (American Library Association, 2002). Published loose-leaf, with quarterly updates. Standard for bibliographic description and analysis for libraries since the 1960s, however catalogers are questioning its relevancy, and alternative standards are being explored.
- *AUTOCAT* (Online discussion group). A semi-moderated list serving the international cataloging community. Subscription information and searchable archives available at ublib.buffalo.edu/libraries/units/cts/autocat
- Calhoun, Karen. *The changing nature of the catalog and its integration with other discovery tools.* Final report. (Library of Congress, 2006). This study, commissioned by the Library of Congress, assesses the effectiveness of current library catalogs, and makes recommendations for a newer model to reflect the information needs of 21st century users. www.loc.gov/catdir/calhoun-report-final. pdf
- *Describing archives: a content standard (DACS).* (Society of American Archivists, 2004.) Revised standard for archival description adapted by US archives, supercedes *Archives, personal papers and manuscripts* (1989).
- *IASA Cataloging rules : a manual for the description of sound recordings and related audiovisual media* / compiled and edited by the IASA Editorial Group convened by Mary Miliano. (Stockholm : IASAA, 1999.) International standard for cataloging sound recordings.

- Library of Congress. *MARC Standards.* Official website for MARC, the internationally recognized bibliographic encoding standard. www.loc.gov/marc
- Matters, Marion. *Oral history cataloging manual.* (Society of American Archivists, 1995). Designed for library catalogers. Many examples in MARC format, applying AACRII rules.
- OCLC. *Bibliographic formats and standards.* MARC format description, as interpreted by OCLC. www.oclc.org/bibformats/default.htm
- *OLAC: online audiovisual catalogers.* Internet and AV Media catalogers network, including an online discussion group. ublib.buffalo.edu/libraries/units/cts/olac
- Plassard, Marie-France, ed. *Functional requirements for bibliographic records : final report. (FRBR).* (Saar, 1998). www.ifla.org/VII/s13/frbr/frbr.pdf
- *Program for cooperative cataloging* (Library of Congress). An international cooperative effort to expand access to library collections. www.loc.gov/catdir.pcc
- *Resources Description Framework* (maintained by W3C). A portal, frequently updated, for RDF development, an area that will increasingly involve traditional catalogers. www.w3.org/RDF
- Tillett, Barbara. *What is FRBR? : a conceptual model for the bibliographic universe.* (Library of Congress, Cataloging Distribution Service, 2004). www.loc.gov/cds/FRBR.html
- Walch, Victoria Irons, comp. *Standards for archival description : a handbook.* (Society of American Archivists, 1994) Online version by Stephen Miller at www.archivists.org/catalog/stds99/index.html

METADATA
- Baca, Murtha, ed. *Introduction to metadata : pathways to digital information.* (Getty Information Institute, 2002)

Best introduction to metadata. www.getty.edu/research/
conducting_research/standards/intrometadata
- Caplan, Priscilla. *Metadata fundamentals for all librarians*. (American Library Association, 2003.)
- *EAD (Encoded Archival Description) Official Website*. EAD documentation, standards, frequent updates and subscription to an online discussion group. www.loc.gov/ead
- METS (Metadata Encoding and Transmission Standard). www.loc.gov/standards.mets
- *Using Dublin Core*. Dublin Core Metadata Initiative, website maintained by Diane Hillmann. Frequently updated user guide. dublincore.org/documents/usageguide

CONTROLLED VOCABULARIES
- *AAT (Art & Architecture Thesaurus)*. www.getty.edu/research/conducting_research/vocabularies/aat
- *ET (Ethnographic Thesaurus)*. In development at the time of this writing, but will be available on the American Folklore Society website, www.afsnet.org; The development group has a website, *Ethnographic thesaurus: a controlled vocabulary ...*, www.afsnet.org/thesaurus
- *Library of Congress Authorities*. Names and subjects. authorities.loc.gov
- *MeSH (Medical Subject Headings)*. www.nlm.nih.gov/mesh
- *TGN (Getty Thesaurus of Geographic Names)*. www.getty.edu/research/conducting_research/vocabularies/tgn

PRESERVATION
- AATA Online (Abstracts of international conservation literature), hosted by the Getty Research Institute. Free to registered users. aata.getty.edu/nps
- Blood, George. *Planning an audio preservation transfer project*. Presentation at the Society of American Archivists meeting, August 23, 2002, rev. January 12, 2005. www.safesoundarchive.com/PDF/AudioPreservProjectPlanning.pdf

- Byers, Fred R. *Care and handling of CDs and DVDs: a guide for librarians and archivists.* (CLIR, 2003). www.clir.org/PUBS/reports/pub121/pub121.pdf
- Casey, Mike and Jon Dunn. *Audio preservation at Indiana University* (PowerPoint Presentation). www.dlib.indiana.edu/workshops/bbspring05slides/audio/casey.ppt
- Casey, Mike. "An overview of worldwide developments in digital preservation of audio," paper presented at the ARSC Conference, April 2, 2005. Available from the author, micasey@indiana.edu
- Dale, Robin, et al. *Audio preservation: a selective annotated bibliography and brief summary of current practices.* (American Library Association, 1998). www.ala.org/ala/alctscontent/alctspubsbucket/webpublications/alctspreservation/audiopreservatio/audiopres.pdf
- *Digital Audio Best Practices.* Version 2.5 (Collaborative Digitization Program, 2005). www.cdpheritage.org/digital/audio/documents/CDPDABP 1-2.pdf
- Fleischhauer, Carl. "Reformatting: a Library of Congress perspective." Paper delivered at the Preservation Conference: Digital Technology vs. Analog Technology, March 27, 2003. www.archives.gov/preservation/conferences/papers-2003/fleischauer.html
- *Folk heritage collections in crisis.* (CLIR, 2001) Based on a conference of the same name convened by the American Folklore Society and the American Folklife Center of the Library of Congress. www.clir.org/pubs/reports/pub96/contents.html
- Hess, Richard. *Restoration tips & notes: media formats & resources.* Audio preservationist provides tips for analog audio restoration, and blog on current topics. richardhess.com/notes/formats

- IASA Technical Committee. *The safeguarding of the audio heritage: ethics, principles and preservation strategy.* (IASA Technical Committee Papers, 2001). www.iasa-web.org/iasa0013.htm
- Kenney, Anne R. and Oya Rieger. *Moving theory into practice: digital imaging for libraries and archives. (RLG, 2000).* Handbook for digitizing cultural resources.
- *LOCKSS (Lots of Copies Keeps Stuff Safe).* Open source software for libraries and archives for preserving and providing access to digital collections. www.lockss.org
- Medina, Larry. "CDs, lies, and magnetic tapes." *Computer World* blog, posted January 10, 2006. www.computerworld.com/blogs/node/1552
- National Archives and Records Administration. *Long-term usability of optical media.* palimpset.stanford.edu/bytopic/electronic-records/electronic-storage-media/cristiss.html
- National Recording Preservation Board (Library of Congress). *Capturing analog sound for digital preservation: report of the roundtable discussion of best practices for transferring analog discs and tapes.* (Library of Congress, CLIR, 2006). www.clir.org/pubs/reports/pub137/pub137.pdf
- *The NINCH guide to good practice in the digital representation and management of cultural heritage materials.* (NINCH, 2002). www.nyu.edu.its/humanities/ninchguide
- Northeast Document Conservation Center. *Assessing preservation needs: a self-survey guide.* www.nedcc.org/selfsurvey/sec2b.htm
- Ogden, Sharon. *Preservation of library and archival materials: a manual.* 3rd ed. (Northeast Document Conservation Center, 1999) www.nedcc.org/plam3/manual.pdf
- *Preservation Reformatting: Digital Technology vs. Analog Technology.* (Preservation and Archives Professionals: 18th Annual Preservation Conference, 2003.) Includes papers by Howard Besser, Steven Puglia, Carl Fleischauer,

and Ed Zwaneveld. www.archives.gov/preservation/conferences/2003

- Smith, Abby, David Randal Allen and Karen Allen. *Survey of the state of audio collections in academic libraries.* (CLIR, 2004) www.clir.org/pubs/reports/pub128/contents.html
- *Sound directions: digital preservation and access for global audio heritage* (Indiana University Archives of Traditional Music and Harvard University's Archive of World Music). dlib.indiana.edu/projects/sounddirections
- *The state of digital preservation: an international perspective.* Conference proceedings: Documentation Abstracts, Inc. & Institutes for Information Science, April 24-25, 2002. (CLIR, 2002). www.clir.org/PUBS/reports/pub107/pub107.pdf
- Stuart, Lynn. *Preservation and access technology: a structured glossary of technical terms.* (CLIR, 1990). www.clir.org/pubs/abstract/pub10.htm.
- *Sustainability of digital formats: planning for Library of Congress collections.* www.digitalpreservation.gov/formats
- van Bogart, John W. C. *Magnetic tape storage and handling: a guide for libraries and archives.* (Commission on Preservation and Access ; National Media Laboratory, 1995). www.clir.org/pubs/reports/pub54

Websites for Preservation

- *ARSC (Association for Recorded Sound Collections).* www.arsc-audio.org
- *Collaborative Digitization Program* (formerly Colorado Digitization Project). Tools and resources for digitizing historical materials. www.cdpheritage.org
- *CoOl (Conservation online: resources for conservation professionals).* Hosted by Stanford University. Portal for preservation and conservation. palimpset.stanford.edu
- *Historical voices.* Tools for preserving and displaying cultural heritage. www.historicalvoices.org
- *Image Permanence Institute.* Hosted by Rochester Institute of Technology. www.imagepermanenceinstitute.org
- *Library of Congress Preservation Portal.* www.loc.gov/preserv

- *National Digital Information and Infrastructure Program (NDIPP).* Coordinates national strategy to collect, archive and preserve digital content. www.digitalpreservation.gov
- Washington State Library. *Digital Best Practices.* digitalwa.statelib.wa.gov/newsite/best.htm

ORAL HISTORIES ON THE INTERNET

- Arms, Caroline R. "Historical collections for the national digital library: lessons and challenges at the Library of Congress," *D-Lib* (April 1996). www.dlib.org/dlib/april96/loc/04c-arms.html
- Cohen, Daniel J. and Roy Rosenzweig. *Digital history : a guide to gathering, preserving and presenting the past on the Web.* (University of Pennsylvania Press, 2006). Available in print and at www.chnm.gmu.edu/digitalhistory
- *A framework of guidance for building good digital collections.* NISO Framework Advisory Group. 2d. ed. (National Information Standards Organization, 2004). www.niso.org/framework/Framework2.html
- *NARA guidance for managing web records.* (National Archives and Records Administration, 2005). www.archives.gov/records-mgmt/pdf/managing-web-records-index.pdf
- *The NINCH guide to good practice in the digital representation and management of cultural heritage materials.* (NINCH, 2002). www.nyu.edu/its/humanities/ninchguide
- Oakland Chinatown Oral History Project. www.oacc.cc/programs/ocohp.html
- "Oral History Online," media review by Michael Frisch, Jennifer Abraham, Jeff Suchanek, and Pamela Dean. *Oral history review.* Vol.32, no.2 (Summer/Fall 2005). Reviews the Alexander Street Press database *Oral History Online.* www.alexanderstreet.com/products/orhi.htm
- Save Our Sounds. www.saveoursounds.org
- Schneider, William. *So they understand: cultural issues in oral history.* (Utah State University Press, 2002). Ethical issues concerning oral histories on the Internet.

- *Sound directions: digital preservation and access for global audio heritage* (Indiana University Archives of Traditional Music and Harvard University's Archive of World Music). dlib.indiana.edu/projects/sounddirections
- Telling Their Stories. www.tellingstories.org

SURVEYS & STUDIES ABOUT ARCHIVED ORAL HISTORIES

- Brewster, Karen. *Internet access to oral recordings: finding the issues.* (Oral History Program, University of Alaska, Fairbanks, 2000). Ethical issues of posting oral histories on the web at: www.uaf.edu/library/oralhistory/brewster1/index.html
- Mackay, Nancy. *Curating oral histories: survey results..* Survey upon which this book is based, concerned with the state of oral histories in archives. www.nancymackay.net/curating/finalSurveyResults.html
- *A public trust at risk: the heritage health index report on the state of America's collections.* (Heritage Preservation with the Institute of Museum and Library Services, 2005). www.heritagepreservation.org/HHI
- Smith, Abby, David Randal Allen and Karen Allen. *Survey of the state of audio collections in academic libraries.* (CLIR, 2004). www.clir.org/pubs/reports/pub128/pub128.pdf
- *Survey of folk heritage collections: summary of results,* American Folklore Society, American Folklife Center of the Library of Congress, and the Society for Ethnomusicology. www.clir.org/pubs/reports/pub96/appendix2.html
- Walch, Virginia Irons. *Where history begins : a report on historical records repositories in the United States.* (Council of State Historical Records Coordinators, 1998). www.statearchivists.org/reports/HRRS/HRRSALL.pdf
- Zorich, Diane. *A survey of Digital Cultural Heritage Initiatives (DCHIs) and their sustainability concerns.* (CLIR, 2003). www.clir.org/pubs/abstract/pub118abst.html

ONLINE PROJECT GUIDES

- *Capturing the living past: an oral history primer*, developed by Barbara Sommer and Mary Kay Quinlan. for the Nebraska State Historical Society, 2005. www.nebraskahistory.org/lib-arch/research/audiovis/oral_history
- *Conducting oral histories.* California Council for the Humanities. www.calhum.org/Resources/oralHistories.htm
- *Handbook for oral history in the National Park Service* (Draft). 2005. www.cr.nps.gov/history/oh/oral.htm
- *Oral history techniques: how to organize and conduct oral history interviews* (Barbara Truesdell, Indiana University Center for the Study of History and Memory). www.indiana.edu/~cshm/techniques.html
- *SOHP how to guide.* Southern Oral History Program (University of North Carolina). www.sohp.org/howto/guide/index.html
- *StoryCorps.* storycorps.net
- *Sunnyvale voices: from settlers to Silicon, project design manual* by Steve Sloan and Tony Calvo. Comprehensive project manual, including budgets, staff needs and lessons learned. sunnyvale.ca.gov/voices/Manual.pdf

ABOUT THE AUTHOR

Angela Zusman (pictured here with her grandmother Claire) has many years experience as an oral historian, writer, editor, book consultant and book artist. Her love of stories inspired her to found the company Uniquely Perfect (www.uniquelyperfect.com) to support individuals, families, communities and organizations in documenting their stories and preserving them in ways that can be shared, such as books, events, and exhibitions. Whenever possible, she travels to teach workshops and offer presentations on the value and process of life-writing to people of all ages. Meanwhile, she is also at work on her own travel memoir.